PUBLIC OPINION POLLING

*A Handbook for Public Interest
and Citizen Advocacy Groups*

Celinda C. Lake

with Pat Callbeck Harper

Montana Alliance for Progressive Policy

ISLAND PRESS

Washington, D.C. □ *Covelo, California*

ABOUT ISLAND PRESS

Island Press publishes, markets, and distributes the most advanced thinking on the conservation of our natural resources — books about soil, land, water, forests, wildlife, and hazardous and toxic wastes. These books are practical tools used by public officials, business and industry leaders, natural resource managers, and concerned citizens working to solve both local and global resource problems.

Founded in 1978, Island Press reorganized in 1984 to meet the increasing demand for substantive books on all resource-related issues. Island Press publishes and distributes under its own imprint and offers these services to other nonprofit research organizations. To date Island Press has worked with a large cross section of the environmental community including: The Nature Conservancy, National Audubon Society, Sierra Club, World Wildlife Fund and The Conservation Foundation, Environmental Policy Institute, Council for Economic Priorities, and National Wildlife Federation.

For additional information about Island Press publishing services and a catalog of current and forthcoming titles contact: Island Press, P.O. Box 7, Covelo, CA 95428.

Funding for the publication of this book was provided by The Beldon Fund, The Field Foundation, and the Northwest Area Foundation.

© 1987 Montana Alliance for Progressive Policy

Library of Congress Cataloging-in-Publication Data

Lake, Celinda C.
    Public opinion polling.

    Bibliography: p.
    Includes index.
    1. Public opinion polls — Handbooks, manuals, etc.
2. Interviewing — Handbooks, manuals, etc.   3. Sampling
(Statistics) — Handbooks, manuals, etc.   I. Harper,
Pat Callbeck.   II. Montana Alliance for Progressive
Policy.   III. Title.
HM261.L18   1987   303.3′8072   87-3157
ISBN 0-933280-32-7

MANUFACTURED IN THE UNITED STATES OF AMERICA

Contents

CHAPTER SIX
Preparing for and Managing Your Interviews   47

CHAPTER SEVEN
Sampling 67

CHAPTER EIGHT
Processing Data: Methods and Options   95

CHAPTER NINE
Analysis   103

CHAPTER TEN
Shortcuts and Pitfalls   **115**

Annotated Bibliography   **123**

Appendices

Acknowledgments

We are grateful foremost to Judy Donald and The Beldon Fund for their generous and patient support of the project that created this book and associated software package for public interest groups.

We also would like to acknowledge the help of Maria Sanchez and the substantial resources and field experience of the Institute for Social Research and The American National Election Studies in helping provide some of the background for the experiences reported in this book.

Much of the information on the new technique of telephone polling also came from a seminar conducted by Charles Cannell and Robert Groves in the summer of 1983 at the Survey Research Center. Conversations with Dr. Cannell and Dr. Groves during the seminar and informally afterward added enormously to our understanding of telephone polling.

We are indebted to Rusty Harper for skillful editing, helpful suggestions, and the clear and creative writing of Chapter 9 on Analysis.

Finally, the authors have conducted numerous polls with public interest groups and campaigns in Michigan, Montana, and Wyoming. We profited enormously from the experiences and hard work of the volunteers and staffs of those organizations, some of whom contributed to this book directly by reviewing it during preparation.

Celinda C. Lake
Pat Callbeck Harper

CHAPTER ONE

Before We Begin . . .

In 1984, polling became a $4-billion-a-year business. Polls help us determine everything, from which dog food people buy to which political candidate they will vote for.

Jimmy Carter probably knew on election eve in 1980 that he would not be reelected because his pollsters had done a good job of predicting.

The editors of *Literary Digest* magazine in 1936, foretelling their demise because of their prediction on the FDR-Landon race, probably wished they had had such good pollsters working for them — they had predicted that Landon would win with 60% of the vote!

Polls are a tremendously valuable tool in today's political world. Our goal with this guidebook and associated software package is to make this tool fully accessible to public interest groups. You need to know how to use this important tool. But first, you need to know what's in this book and how to use it.

THE USES OF THIS BOOK

There are two major uses for this guidebook:

1. To help you plan and complete a professional poll.
2. To help you become a wise consumer of polls for your own and your organization's best interests.

This book presents hands-on information on how to plan, administer, and analyze a poll. And because polls can be used

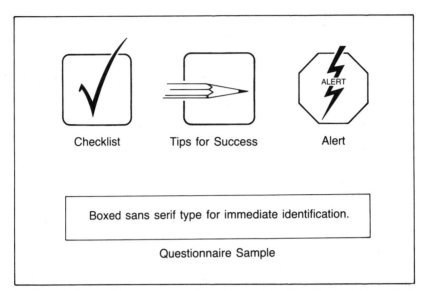

FIGURE 1-1 *Graphic conventions to help you are used throughout this book.*

against you, this book also helps you to analyze the sampling, interpretation, and question-wording of polls conducted by other
orgnizations.

The text includes examples, checklists, warnings of possible
pitfalls, and lists of additional material and human resources to help
you in your polling efforts. Samples of most of the materials you will
need to produce a poll are also included.

The software package POLLSTART, its manual, and this book
give you a complete package for polling that takes you from sampling through analysis. More information on POLLSTART is found
in Appendix F. This book also is designed to be used on its own without the software package.

Some polling manuals tell you just enough to conduct your poll
but don't explain the theory or logic behind this tool. This often
means that any adjustments you may make can unwittingly endan-
ger the quality of your poll. Other textbooks are too complex,
detailed, and lengthy to be used well and easily by public and citizen
interest groups. This book strikes a middle ground.

HOW TO USE THIS BOOK

You might ask, "Why not just pick a chapter and start polling?"
Since the results of this important scientific tool could be very

important to your work and your organization, we suggest that you read the book through completely. A good understanding of polling and the choices you must make before you begin will reap benefits for you later.

The chapters will walk you through the rationale and the steps in polling. Most chapters end with a checklist of questions that you need to answer before going on to the next stage. Suggestions of community resources for additional help are also noted.

If you are using this book primarily as a consumer of polls, you will want to concentrate on the chapters on sampling, questionnaire construction, and analysis. By using the suggestions and checklists provided in this book, you are certain to become a more skilled user and consumer of polls to your benefit and that of your organization.

CHAPTER TWO

Introduction to Polling

LET'S START AT THE BEGINNING—WHAT IS A POLL?

A poll is a systematic, scientific, and impartial way of collecting information from a subset, or **sample,** of people that is used to generalize to a greater group, or **population,** from which the sample was drawn. A poll is not designed to persuade or identify individuals —there are cheaper and more efficient ways of doing that (telephone canvass, for example). Confusing these goals with those of a poll can seriously bias the information you receive. A poll also is not intended to describe any one individual in depth. Again, a case study is a cheaper and more efficient way to do that. A poll is a measurement at one point in time that reveals attitudes, behaviors, beliefs, attributes, and the interrelationship of all of these parameters. These generalizations can then be extended to the larger society.

In a poll, information is obtained in a scientific, controlled way from a selected subset of people.

A properly selected subset enables you to generalize your findings reliably to a greater population (without talking to everyone) after attributing a known margin of error to the sampling. Careful interviewing, questionnaire construction, and analysis also minimize other forms of error that are difficult to measure.

Because a poll is not designed to influence or persuade people, you should never identify your organization or goals in such a way as to influence your respondents' answers. The interviewing should be kept as neutral as possible.

WHAT ARE THE VALUES OF POLLING?

To give you an idea of how valuable a poll can be to your organization, we have listed some of the kinds of information a poll can help you obtain. Polls can help you determine:

☐ **What people are thinking** — what they see as important problems, what their opinions on policy and issue questions are, what tradeoffs they are willing to make in policy and budgetary decisions, what they think are appropriate arenas for public involvement, and how they want to see resources allocated.

☐ **What people know** — what political figures and groups they are aware of, which issues and arguments about issues are important to them, and what factual information they have.

☐ **How people perceive issues and political objects** — how they evaluate their political figures' and institutions' performances, what emotional attachment they have for groups and individuals, for whom they would vote, and what reactions they have to certain slogans or information about political figures and issues.

☐ **Characteristics of people** — what their social and political characteristics are, how interested they are in a topic or event, and where they get their information on different topics.

The most valuable aspect of polling, however, is not just looking at these parameters individually, but rather linking them — seeing who feels what, where they live, how they can be reached, what points are important to them, and what issues are linked for them.

Examining the **covariance,** or linkage of opinions with other attitudes and social and political characteristics, reveals why certain beliefs are held, as well as what beliefs are held. This information can be used to develop strategies for influencing public opinion, political events, and political figures. You can target groups by issue and demographic characteristics. You can discuss or confront issues with an awareness of how those issues are actually perceived by different groups.

Polls have tremendous internal value for your group in developing strategies and assessing the impact of strategy and events. They also can be used externally. Polls can be released as the basis for news items; they also can be used to obtain money, political support, and media attention by demonstrating the viability of your ideas or candidacy. Polls can be used to influence the behavior of public officials or rally the support of your volunteers. They can be a service you exchange with allied groups or political candidates . . . and much, much more.

There are many situations in which a public interest group might want to conduct a survey using volunteers. For example, you might want to contribute this as an in-kind service to a candidate who supports your issues. You might use a poll to target a bad incumbent, using the results to develop strategies for recruiting a challenger and defeating the incumbent. You might want to bring an issue to people's attention, but before you do so you may need to measure what people believe and why they hold those beliefs.

After a press or grassroots strategy, you might want to measure whether and how much attitudes have changed to plan your next move and assess your success. Survey data may make news and persuade officials, even when the survey is conducted by volunteers.

This book will help you not only to conduct polls, but also to analyze the results of polls conducted by other groups. Other groups may use their poll results to undermine your efforts. It is important that you be able to evaluate the validity of their results to determine your own strategy and counter their efforts. Because different results frequently are released by different groups, you should be able to evaluate the wording of the questions, methodology, and sampling.

Only with a basic understanding of polling methods can you be an informed reader and purchaser of polls. Today, everyone is affected by polls, and this book is an important resource regardless of whether we're conducting or being influenced by them.

WHAT TYPES OF POLLS ARE THERE?

There are four basic types of polls: in-depth surveys, short polls, tracking polls, and panels.

In-depth surveys, the most common type of poll, are 20-60 minute surveys that assess public opinion on one or more topics in depth. This type of survey sometimes can serve as a benchmark when followed by **short polls,** 10-15 minute surveys that assess change over time and the impact of events and strategy.

A **tracking poll** is used to assess a rapidly changing trend occurring over a short period of time. This type of poll, which often is used at the end of a political campaign, for example, asks a few key questions of a small sample (100-200 people) in 5-10 minutes at short intervals (for example, every other night).

If you are interested in understanding change and why it occurred, you need to conduct a **panel poll,** in which you interview the same people at two different points in time. Asking the same individuals similar questions at two different times enables you to make some assessments regarding changes in opinion, as well as determine some of the reasons for the change. Panel polls often are used to assess the effectiveness of a public education campaign to influence opinion or knowledge on an issue.

DEBUNKING SOME MYTHS ABOUT POLLS

Myth No. 1: "Volunteers cannot conduct good polls."

Good polls can be conducted by volunteers at almost every stage. As in any volunteer task, however, the volunteers must be well trained, understand what they are doing, and be well supervised.

It is essential that someone with a good understanding of polling be in charge of the poll. It's also helpful to identify some polling experts in the community who can answer the questions that invariably arise.

The most successful polling efforts frequently are achieved when the volunteers have a sense of ownership for the task. Volunteers should be recruited for the task in the early stages, see the poll through to the end, be delegated distinct responsibilities, and be supplemented by other volunteers as needed.

Myth No. 2: "Polling is too complex and costly for public interest groups."

In fact, with donated services and local calls, a poll can require little actual cash outlay. Money will be needed to pay for photocopying questionnaires and lists of registered voters, getting telephone directories, or using a computer to obtain telephone numbers. The major (and potentially costly) tasks of typing, sampling, interviewing, questionnaire writing, planning, analysis, data management, and training, however, theoretically can all be done by existing staff or volunteers. These tasks will be time-consuming, of course, especially if done by volunteers. A key factor in doing an in-house poll is to allow ample time, particularly for the first stages.

If you are planning to conduct anything lengthier than a 10-minute poll, you also may have to pay for data analysis.

The POLLSTART software package that can be used with this book is designed for direct data entry from your questionnaires and has safeguards against "invalid punches." This software is designed for easy, accurate data entry by volunteers and can be used on most personal computers. Given the widespread availability of personal computers, someone in your group probably will have access to a system with the equipment needed to print all of your poll analyses.

As discussed in Chapter 5 on Interviewing, interviewing from a central location is infinitely preferable to having volunteers operate from their own homes. Law offices, banks, construction firms, union halls, or even your own office are good places to start looking for a telephone bank. Keep in mind while searching that you will be calling after working hours. To avoid long-distance calling, you may want to establish telephone centers in several cities with supervisors for each.

To conduct a quality poll, you need to plan ahead. You will need someone to supervise the poll, someone to coordinate volunteers, and someone to take care of data entry. A volunteer poll usually requires a core of three to five people, at least 20 people willing to do the interviewing, and two to three volunteers for data entry. Although advance planning is needed, these volunteer requirements are usually well within the reach of most public interest groups.

Myth No. 3: "Anyone can do a 'quick and dirty' poll."

Polling is not complex, but it is a precise exercise, with many steps leading to the finished product. It requires detailed planning, careful supervision, attention to detail, and a great deal of time. During some stages, it also can demand substantial volunteer time.

No one can do a perfect study, but this book is designed to help you conduct the best poll possible. This book helps you identify your goals and resources and recognize the tradeoffs inherent in the decisions you must make. This book should give you a thorough enough understanding of the polling process to: (1) implement the necessary steps efficiently; (2) conduct a survey at minimal cost; and (3) be fully aware of the nature of what you are beginning. Well-organized polls are enormously useful to an organization, as well as interesting for the people involved. Polls are also a great way of using the talents of the people who support your organization.

CHAPTER THREE

Getting Started

WHAT'S IT ALL ABOUT?

The first step in any poll is to determine the **study objective** — what information you want and how you plan to use it. Your objectives should be clear, and every question should contribute to them. Think about what information you want, how you plan to use it, and then consider what questions you need to ask to both understand and utilize your findings. Study objectives may include questions that help you:

- ☐ Separate people into political, social, and issue target groups.
- ☐ Determine how best to use the media to reach your groups.
- ☐ Identify "intervening attitudes," that is, factors that influence the relationship you are studying, so you know something about how people form their opinions.

As soon as you know what you want to ask, it will become clear who you want to ask — that is, your target population. Your target population may be all registered voters, all people in a geographic area, all likely voters, all members of an organization, and so on.

Planning the who, what, where, when, and how of the survey is called laying out the **study design.** A detailed plan will help you determine what people you need at what times and what tasks have to be completed by what time so that the next task can begin. The case study presented in Appendix E will help you plan your study.

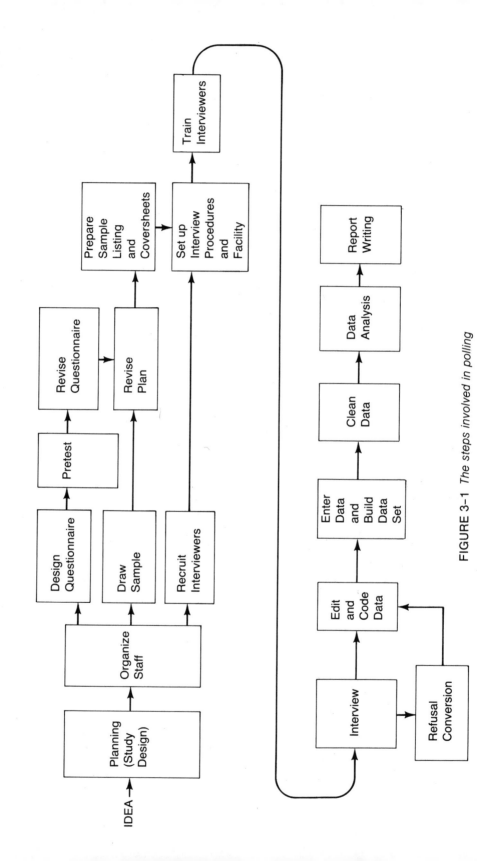

FIGURE 3–1 *The steps involved in polling*

This book also goes into more detail about each of the steps in subsequent chapters. Figure 3-1 is a flowchart showing the steps in a poll.

Once you know who you want to interview and what you want to ask them, you are ready to determine what type of poll you want to use. There are three possible methods of polling: by telephone, in person, and by mail. All three methods of polling have tradeoffs in terms of cost, types of resources needed, coverage of the population, response rate (the number of eligible sampled people who generate completed interviews), types of questions that can be asked, control over the interview, ease of administration, types of training needed, and type and amount of error incurred.

This book focuses on telephone interviewing, although many of the chapters, such as those on questionnaire wording and analysis, would apply largely to all methods of polling. As a user of polls, comparing the advantages and disadvantages of the different methods will help you determine whether the best method has been chosen. For example, one might suspect sampling bias in a telephone survey of rural, black farmers in Mississippi because a high proportion of potential respondents might not have a telephone.

The following is a brief discussion of the advantages and disadvantages of mail and personal interviewing, as well as a more in-depth look at telephone interviews. Table 3-1 gives a quick comparison of interviewing methods, one of the areas of greatest difference among the methods.

MAIL SURVEYS

Advantages

Groups often favor mail surveys because they are inexpensive and require a minimum of personnel and organization. Mail surveys also make it relatively easy to ask complex questions because the questions are in front of the respondent.

Disadvantages

The response rate on mail interviews is low, often around 30%, if the initial mailings are not followed with reminders. In turn, the mailing of reminders increases costs and the administrative task of keeping track of the sample. The low response rate is accentuated by poor sample coverage. It is difficult to get a complete, accurate mailing list for any population. Furthermore, with unreturned mail surveys, it is difficult to determine whether the respondent ever received the survey or if he or she chose not to respond.

It also is difficult to control the respondent behavior when using a mail survey. For example, it is impossible to clarify questions, explain procedures, probe for more complete answers, control the question order, or control who answers the questions.

PERSONAL SURVEYS

Advantages

Personal surveys are generally considered the best for obtaining in-depth and complex information and for controlling the interview. Because the interviewer is present and can use both visual and verbal cues, almost any type of question can be asked.

Personal surveys tend to yield higher-quality answers because respondents work harder, concentrate more, and give more detailed responses. Longer surveys (over an hour) also are better conducted in person than by other methods.

Personal surveys also maximize sample coverage because interviewers actually go out and list the sample. One need not worry about the quality or newness of a list or whether the respondent has a telephone or mailbox. The physical presence of an interviewer with credentials does much to establish the legitimacy of the poll, and in the past, response rates were highest for personal interviews. Recently, however, people, especially those in urban areas, have become frightened of letting strangers into their homes, and as a result, response rates for personal interviews in urban areas have fallen. The response rates for telephone and personal surveys are now about the same (65–75%).

Disadvantages

Cost is the major disadvantage of personal surveys. In addition to cost, the demands of recruiting interviewers, supervising them, and administering the survey increase rapidly as the sample becomes more geographically dispersed.

TABLE 3-1 *Evaluating Interviewing Methods* [a, b]

Task	Telephone	Personal	Mail
Administration			
Cost	2	4	1
Time to implement	1	4	4
Staff needed	3	4	1
Sampling			
Population covered	2	1	2
Ability to obtain population list	2	1	3
Control over selection of respondent in household and non-substitution of respondents	2	1	4
Interviewing			
Respondent response rate	2	1	4
Respondent refusal rate	2	2	(Can't determine)
Supervision of interviewers	1	3	—
Ability of interviewer to probe	2	1	4
Ability of interviewer to clarify	2	1	4
Avoid social desirability in responses	3	4	1
Avoid interviewer contamination	2	3	1
Avoid skipping questions (item nonresponse)	2	1	4
Questionnaire			
Length of questionnaire	2	1	3
Type of question			
Success of open-ended questions	2	1	4
Success of complex questions	3	1	2
Success controlling sequence of questions	1	1	4

[a]The scale used in this table runs from 1 (strong *relative* advantage) to 4 (strong *relative* disadvantage).
[b]This table relies extensively on ideas discussed by Frey, 1983 and Dillman, 1978.

TELEPHONE SURVEYS

Advantages

Telephone surveys have the fastest turnaround time of all the polling methods. They can cost up to 50% less than personal surveys for commercial polls and yield good-quality data for the money.

Telephone surveys also are slightly easier to administer and require somewhat fewer interviewers, particularly if a centralized telephone bank is used. In addition, interviewers in telephone surveys have almost as much control over respondent selection as personal interviewers, although it can be more difficult to obtain a listing of household members over the telephone than it is in person because some people, particularly senior citizens and single women, are nervous about giving such information to someone they do not know and cannot see.

Although telephone interviewers must rely solely on verbal cues, their ability to probe, clarify, and reinforce answers is not hampered. There also is less interviewer contamination over the telephone than in person because the interviewer's behavior is better controlled through more immediate and direct supervision. Because respondents cannot see interviewers, they tend to refrain from making judgments about what the interviewers are like and what answers they would prefer to receive.

Disadvantages

Lack of coverage is a major disadvantage of telephone surveys. According to the U.S. Census Bureau and other survey estimates, about 5% of the U. S. population does not have a telephone. (Five states have less than 90% coverage.) People without telephones tend to be less affluent, younger, more mobile, rent rather than own their dwellings, and live in rural areas. Unmarried men and minorities are also more likely to lack telephones than others.

Sampling from telephone directories is biased by unlisted numbers, duplicate listings, out-of-date listings, and nonworking numbers. People with unlisted numbers tend to be female, Republican, older, long-term residents, urban dwellers, and in some urban areas working-class members of ethnic groups. These problems are discussed in more detail in Chapter 7 on Sampling.

The length of interviews is also more limited over the telephone, although not as limited as one might expect. With well-trained interviewers, the telephone can be used successfully for up to 45-minute interviews. After 45 minutes, the number of partial interviews, those where respondents quit in the middle, increases. However, successful interviews lasting as long as 65 minutes can be conducted with the general population over the telephone.

Poorly conducted telephone interviewing has a greater tendency to yield low-quality data than does personal interviewing because respondents do not concentrate as well and become confused more easily with only telephone contact.

Finally, there is a limit to the complexity of questions that can be asked over the telephone because a respondent can only remember and grasp so much without visual aids. Also, open-ended questions elicit shorter answers over the telephone than they do in person.

 CHECKLIST—GETTING STARTED

1. What information do I want?
2. How do I plan to use it?
3. What is my target population?
4. What method of polling am I going to use?
5. What is my study design?
6. How am I going to sample my target population?
7. What am I going to ask?
8. When am I going to interview?
9. Who is going to conduct the interviews?
10. Have I set up a plan of chronological steps (flowchart) with resources needed and tasks that must be performed — and the deadlines for meeting these needs?

CHAPTER FOUR

Questionnaire Wording and Construction

INTRODUCTION

More than any other section of the polls, question writing and designing and constructing the questionnaire involve both art and science. There should be a specific reason for every question asked because unnecessary questions waste time, money, and energy. All questions should fit into the overall purpose of the poll. Don't ask something just because it is interesting.

The only way to write clear, unambiguous questions is to be clear beforehand about what you want to learn from each question. Questions are poorly worded when they are unclear, too broad, ambiguous, or assume too much knowledge on the part of the respondent. Poor question wording can have extremely harmful effects on your results by introducing a degree of error that is impossible to measure. Poor question wording can encourage certain answers, discourage others, confuse respondents, and generally bias results. Questions are biased when one answer is more likely to be chosen than another because of the wording.

Question wording is particularly important in telephone interviewing, where communication is completely verbal and questions need to be less complex and more repetitious. Question wording can introduce tremendous changes in poll results. As a consumer of polls, you also will want to pay particular attention to the sequence of questions, the wording, and the response categories offered.

This chapter covers not only question wording, but questionnaire construction, including instructions for the interviewers, transitions between questions, and the sequence of questions.

TYPES OF QUESTIONS

There are two basic types of questions — open-ended and close-ended questions. Each type of question is useful for obtaining different types of information and performing different kinds of analyses.

Close-ended Versus Open-ended Questions

Close-ended questions offer respondents a choice among two or a few answers. For example:

> Are you a citizen of this country — yes or no?
>
> How often do you attend concerts in the park — daily, weekly, at least once a year, or never?

Close-ended questions are the quickest to ask and easiest to answer because they require little thought on the part of the respondents. They simply pick from the answers offered. Close-ended questions ensure that all the responses are similar. They also do not need to be "coded," or lumped into categories for purposes of analysis.

Open-ended questions allow people to respond in their own words. For example:

> What do you feel is the most important problem currently facing Montana?

Interviewers record the exact response, which is later coded in certain categories. Open-ended questions are useful when you want to see how respondents discuss an issue or discover what is on their minds without imposing an agenda. Open-ended questions are really exploratory questions that are used when you don't know how a person will respond or when you don't want to limit responses by imposing a set of categories. Open-ended questions allow more spontaneous responses. For example, they are useful when looking for preconceptions and any likes or dislikes people may have about your group.

Open-ended questions, which are more difficult to ask, answer, and analyze, are commonly overused. These questions only work when the topic is relevant to the respondent, and the interviewers are trained to probe and reinforce respondents, so the latter know when they have given a complete answer.

Writing Good Questions Requires Expertise

Questionnaire construction is much more complex than most people believe. A good, unbiased questionnaire cannot be cranked out in ten minutes. Many groups have experienced people to look at their sampling technique but fail to do the same with the questionnaire. People in state government, local party organizations, universities, personnel departments of businesses and banks, and union organizations often have the experience to evaluate the wording of your questionnaire.

HOW DO YOU WORD QUESTIONS?

There are a variety of things to watch for in question wording. In this section, we will briefly discuss these problem areas and include a checklist at the end. Appendix B gives examples of questions worded to avoid common problems.

Vocabulary

Questions should be grammatically correct and avoid the use of jargon or complex vocabulary. Don't use slang or folksy phrases. Your goal is to use words that are clear and unambiguous and have the same meaning to all the people interviewed. Here are some things to remember:

- ☐ The question should have a clear time frame, such as "this year" or "in the last four years." The phrase conveying the sense of time should come at the beginning of the question so respondents can keep it in mind while they are thinking about the question.
- ☐ You want to be specific without sounding condescending. Don't overelaborate commonly understood concepts. For example, the following question is overelaborated: "Do you think that state property taxes, that is, the taxes you pay Montana on your house, are . . .?"
- ☐ However, don't forget that even the most common phrases often can be misinterpreted. In one experiment, Belsan (1981) found that when people were given a question about children, 18% excluded those aged 10 years or less, 36% excluded those over 10, 9% excluded those over 16, and

33% responded by giving some other grouping. Obviously, you can't define every concept in a question, but you should decide what needs to be included so that all respondents are answering the same question.

☐ The answer categories should be as clear and specific as the questions. For example, the response categories on a question about the performance of the U.S. Department of Commerce should not be, "Good," "Fine," "Okay," "Poor." Such categories are distinguished insufficiently from one another, and categories like "fine" are unclear.

☐ In the average survey, the vocabulary should be geared toward respondents with no more than a high school education. Also, bear in mind that unfamiliar words are even more difficult to understand over the telephone than in person.

Length of Questions

If a question is too long, it can be misunderstood. Respondents often forget the early phrases. Clear, simple question wording usually leads to shorter questions.

On the other hand, longer questions sometimes increase the quantity and quality of the response. They give respondents time to think, which is particularly important in telephone interviews. Respondents also tend to give more importance to longer questions and answer them more carefully. In particular, longer questions improve the responses to threatening or sensitive questions. Finally, longer questions will be needed to explain more complicated concepts or provide adequate response scales.

As a general rule, the best way to maximize question length is to allow the most important, sensitive, or complex questions to be longer and have no more than every fourth question be lengthy.

One Question at a Time

Each question should only ask one thing at a time. A poorly written question sometimes implies the answer to a previous question. For example:

> Do you favor reducing Americans' use of gasoline by increasing our taxes on foreign oil?

A person who answers "No" could be referring to not favoring reducing the use of gasoline or to favoring the reduction but not by raising taxes.

In this example, you probably should ask whether Americans' use of gas should be reduced, and then ask one or more follow-up questions about how this should be accomplished. Another method is to establish that if a policy of gasoline reduction must be created, would the respondent favor such and such a means (Weisberg and Bowen, 1977).

In short, a question should never ask two things at once because you will be unsure what the respondent meant by the answer.

Avoid Assumptions

You should avoid questions that assume too much knowledge on the part of the respondent or assume that the respondent holds a particular opinion or has behaved in a certain way. The following are examples of poor questions:

> Do you approve of Ed Weber's stand on the wild horse controversy?
>
> When you drive to work, which radio station do you listen to?

The first question assumes too much knowledge by assuming the respondent knows Weber's position and is aware of the wild horse controversy. The second question assumes a certain behavior, in this case that the respondent drives to work and listens to the radio.

These questions still can be used, but special handling is needed. One technique is to use a filter question, such as:

> Have you heard or read anything about Ed Weber and the wild horse controversy?

This type of question filters out individuals who know nothing about it.

As another approach, you could be sure that all the respondents have the same information. For example:

> Mayor Ed Weber is in favor of running a herd of wild horses in Main Park. Do you approve or disapprove of his plan?

This technique should not be overused, however. In general, you want to ask questions about things on which people have opinions, rather than creating opinions during the interview by providing new information.

Purely hypothetical questions, in which you must provide some new information before the respondent can answer, often produce unstable answers, meaning that the answers are likely to be quite different the next time the respondent is asked. These questions can be desirable in some instances, however, such as determining whether a certain message would be persuasive if it were widely publicized. Respondents need to be "grounded" in common information before they can answer these questions effectively. For example:

> If you knew that _____, would that make you more or less _____?
>
> If you knew that the budget would be balanced by cutting Social Security, would that make you more or less likely to favor a requirement for a balanced budget?

When a question assumes too much knowledge, the respondent often will express a general belief on the subject when replying. In that event, you are better off asking about the general belief, changing your question, or dropping it altogether. For example, if you ask the question, "Do you think the price of zinc has gone up in the last 6 months?"—most people will respond by telling you what they think has happened to prices in general in the last 6 months. If you really want to know their opinions about prices in general, that's what you should ask them. Otherwise, you need to ask a filter question to sort out respondents who know anything about zinc prices.

Questions that include assumptions about people's opinions or ask more than one thing at once often include false tradeoffs. For example:

> Do you think the United States should suspend worker safety regulations to promote economic development?

This assumes there is a connection between the two items. When a person answers "No," they could oppose suspending the regulations despite the promotion of development, they could be denying that suspending the regulations has anything to do with development, or they could be saying that they oppose any action that leads to further development.

The question has two assumptions — that safety regulations are related to economic development and that the respondent favors such development. Because of this, you have no way of knowing by this question alone what the respondent is really thinking.

Repetition

You should avoid a series of questions which differ only slightly in ways that seem important to you but which may be too subtle for the average respondent. If respondents think they are answering essentially the same question, they will be reluctant to continue the interview. Bear in mind that it is particularly difficult to communicate subtle differences between questions over the phone. Respondents tend to concentrate less in such interviews than they do in personal interviews.

For example, if you were asking the general population a series of questions about how the Environmental Protection Agency is performing, you would need to remember the limited amount of information most people will have about different aspects of the agency. A series of questions asking about "fiscal management," "overall administration," and "spending levels" would be redundant for most respondents. Often, series of repetitious questions appear in polls because the pollsters could not decide how best to ask something or were not clear about what they were looking for. Pretesting questions and thinking through the overall goal of the poll and how each question should contribute will help eliminate this kind of repetition. Be sure to allow enough time (at least 24 hours) to adequately pretest and revise your questionnaire. This is a critical stage in questionnaire writing that will save time and energy in the end.

"Don't Know"

You should have a "Don't know" category in your set of answers for almost every question, even if it isn't asked. Groups often resist this rule in the mistaken belief that everyone has an opinion and simply must be coaxed into giving it.

When you include "Don't know" in the answers offered to respondents, the proportion of people using it will increase because you have legitimized admitting that they have no opinion on the issue. Adding such a category usually clarifies what opinions really are held. When people are encouraged to give an opinion on a subject about which they know little or have no opinion, they respond randomly, which tells us very little.

Loaded Questions

 A question that has one answer that is obviously more prestigious, more socially desirable, or reflects the status quo is a **loaded question.** For example:

> When the election is held, will you vote for the current mayor, Judy Smith, or the challenger, Bob Jones?

People who do not have a strong opinion will tend to answer for the incumbent.

The tone of certain words also can load the question. In a famous experiment, half the respondents were asked, "Do you think the United States should allow public speeches against democracy?", whereas the other half were asked, "Do you think the United States should forbid speeches against democracy?" Of the first group, 44% said such speeches should not be allowed, but only 28% of the second group said they should be forbidden (Schuman and Presser, 1981).

Balanced Questions

To get accurate answers, your questions must be **balanced,** which means that both sides of an issue must be presented with equal weight. Unbalanced questions skew the answers, but you have no way of knowing how much. The following unbalanced question, "Would you favor a law that would require a person to obtain a police permit before buying a gun?" will get much higher rate of agreement than the balanced question, "Would you favor a law that would require a person to obtain a police permit before buying a gun, or do you think such a law would interfere too much with the rights of citizens to own guns?" (Schuman and Presser, 1981).

Simply adding the phrase "or not" to the end of a question does not balance it — the alternative must be stated clearly and with equal weight.

Response Categories

Earlier in the chapter we emphasized the pitfalls in wording questions. The wording of answers must also be approached with care. The categories need to be exhaustive and mutually exclusive. They should not be so subtle that respondents can't differentiate between them. Respondents should feel they fit into one and only one category. Respondents also should be able to remember the full range of possible answers. In a telephone interview, this means limiting the possible answers to three to five categories.

Incremental scales are often used because they are easy to remember. Such scales should have categories of equal distance, however. For example, the categories "excellent," "fair," or "poor" are not of equal distance. The categories "good," "fair," or "poor" make a better scale. Middle categories should be used to reflect true opinions. If there is no middle category, many respondents will try to volunteer them anyway. For example, in one experiment, respondents were asked:

> Looking back, do you think our government did too much to help the South Vietnamese government in the war or not enough to help?

In this case, 71% responded "too much," and 11% volunteered "the right amount." When "the right amount" was specifically added as a category, 62% said "too much," and 29% said "the right amount" — a very different distribution (Schuman and Presser, 1981).

Don't Forget the Respondent

Your respondent has to remember the question, think of the answer, and fit that answer into the categories you have given. It helps to repeat the answer scale at the end of the question and also to group together questions that use the same response scale. However, beware of fatiguing respondents by having too many of the same kind of question in a row.

If you want to use a particularly long scale over the telephone, you will have to resort to an **unfolding technique,** in which your first question broadly categorizes people and your follow-up question differentiates them further. A common example is to ask whether you approve or disapprove of X, with the follow-up question asking how strongly you feel.

The longer the survey, the more aware you should be of the respondent's needs. Short polls are used to obtain a quick reading of opinion. Longer polls are used to explore topics in depth, plan strategy, and fully understand opinions on a topic.

Acquiescence Bias

Acquiescence bias means that people tend to agree with questions on which they don't have an opinion. If you use agree/disagree questions, be sure to vary the questions so that no demographic or political group of respondents will always agree with the series.

 CHECKLIST—BASIC QUESTION WORDING

1. Questions should be conversational but not slangy.
2. Wording should be clear and unambiguous so that questions have a single, common meaning for respondents.
3. Use familiar vocabulary.
4. Alternate long and short questions. The most important questions and the ones that require the most thought should be longer.
5. Each question should ask only one thing.
6. Questions should not assume too much respondent knowledge nor an existing opinion.
7. Avoid loaded phrases. In particular, avoid phrases that suggest a certain response is socially desirable or maintains the status quo.
8. Avoid questions that are too similar.
9. In most cases, remember to offer "Don't know" alternatives to questions.
10. Write substantively balanced questions offering alternatives that are given equal weight.
11. Watch the tone of the wording to avoid loading the questions.
12. The answer categories should be easy to remember, of equal distance, exhaustive, and mutually exclusive.
13. Vary agree/disagree questions to avoid acquiescence bias.

HOW DO YOU ARRANGE THE ORDER OF THE QUESTIONNAIRE?

Question Order

Writing the questionnaire is only half the battle. The questions need to be ordered to create a coherent whole that flows well and promotes accurate responses.

The first questions should be easy to answer, nonthreatening, and fairly neutral in content. This convinces the respondents that answering the questions isn't hard. Longer questions can be mixed in after the first few minutes of the interview.

The demographic questions (age, sex, etc.) should come at the end of the survey. If income is asked, it should be last because that question has the highest refusal rate. Questions about religious affiliation also often bring refusals.

In general, sensitive questions should be asked no sooner than the middle of the questionnaire to allow time to establish rapport. Early questions establish the tone of the survey and also give the respondent some reference about what the "real" topic of the survey is.

Questions should be grouped by topic to contribute to the sense of having a conversation with the respondent. Jumping from topic to topic is confusing. Transitions should be neutral such as, "Now for a slightly different topic . . ."

The Effect of the Context

Each question provides the context and information for the next question. Even if you do not see the questions as linked, respondents take cues as to what are desirable, good, or consistent answers from previous questions.

In general, questions should move from open-ended to close-ended on a given topic and from the general to the specific. Asking general questions first gets the respondent thinking about the topic. Asking the specific question first more narrowly focuses and constrains the answer for the following general question. The **subtraction effect** also often occurs when respondents answer a second, more general, question with reference to the general category minus the part they have already responded to in the first question.

As another general rule, *recognition questions should come before candidate preference questions.* Candidate approval and party identification questions should be separated from candidate preference or ballot questions.

 In short, try to avoid situations where respondents feel required to answer a specific way to a question because of the way they responded to a previous question.

HOW DO YOU DESIGN A QUESTIONNAIRE WITH ALL THE "AUDIENCES" IN MIND?

Questionnaires need to be written and printed with the interviewer, coder, and data entry person in mind, as well as the respondent. You should include instructions, probes, and transitions for your interviewers. The questionnaire should be easy to mark. Ample space should be provided to write in the answers to open-ended questions.

The format for each question should be standardized. Anything the interviewer does not read aloud, such as instructions and coding categories, should be capitalized. Avoid abbreviations — spell out words exactly as the interviewer is to read them.

Questions and response categories should never be split across two pages. Series of questions using the same scale should use grids. See examples of this in Appendix B.

Arrows and instructions are needed for questions in which respondents who answer one way are then asked a different follow-up question from respondents who give a different answer. Questions that can be skipped or not asked of some respondents should be boxed off.

In setting up response categories, codes should be reserved for "Don't know." The option "Don't know" sometimes is included in the question as asked, and other times it is not.

Each question also should have a response code for missing data. Missing data codes include "Not applicable" (for example, if a question were skipped by design) and "Not ascertained" for incorrectly skipped questions.

Figure 4-1 shows the first page of a questionnaire that follows these conventions and has been set up for use with POLLSTART, the software package that can be used to supplement this book.

INTERVIEWER NAME _____ DATE _____ INTERVIEW NO. _____

Hello, my name is _____. I'm calling for National Opinion Research Poll, an independent public opinion organization. We're doing a survey in Montana about issues and problems facing the state. Your name was randomly selected from the telephone book to participate in this survey. We will only take a few minutes of your time to talk with you and the answers you give will be kept strictly confidential.

Q1. What do you personally feel is the most important problem currently facing Montana?
Q2. Anything else?

(*DO NOT READ LIST*. WRITE RESPONSE BELOW. DO NOT CHECK THE BOXES—THEY WILL BE CODED LATER.)

1. First mention _____
2. Second mention _____

○ 1.1 INFLATION	○ 1.6 TAXES
○ 1.2 JOBS AND UNEMPLOYMENT	○ 1.7 AGRICULTURE
○ 1.3 ENERGY	○ 1.8 INTEREST RATES
○ 1.4 ENVIRONMENT	○ 1.9 GENERAL ECONOMY
○ 1.5 GOVERNMENT SPENDING	○ 1.10 OTHER _____ (WRITE THE ANSWER)

○ 1.98 DON'T KNOW
○ 1.99–MISSING

In the next few questions, I'm going to read you some choices about issues currently facing Montana, and I'd like you to tell me which answer best describes how you feel:

Q3. Many people have been comparing the quality of Montana's public schools today with the quality of education they received as a child. In general, do you think the education most Montana children get in the public schools is *better, about the same,* or *worse* than the education you received as a child?

○ 3.1 BETTER
○ 3.2 SAME
○ 3.3 WORSE
○ 3.98 DON'T KNOW
○ 3.99–MISSING

Q4. Parents who send their children to private and parochial schools must pay tuition. Would you *favor* or *oppose* giving these

FIGURE 4-1 *National Opinion Research Poll*

parents a break in their income tax for this tuition, or haven't you thought much about this?

┌ + - ○ 4.1   FAVOR—GO TO Q. 5
│   ○ 4.2   OPPOSE—(SKIP TO QUESTION 6)
│   ○ 4.98 DON'T KNOW, HAVEN'T THOUGHT MUCH
│   ABOUT THIS—(SKIP TO QUESTION 6)
↓   ○ 4.99—MISSING

Q5. Would you favor an income tax break for such tuition even if it reduced the money available for public schools?

○ 5.1   YES
○ 5.2   NO
○ 5.98 DON'T KNOW
○ 5.99—MISSING (NOT APPLICABLE)

FIGURE 4-1 *National Opinion Research Poll (continued)*

Finally, it is most desirable to have a copy of the questionnaire for each interview and to mark the respondents' answers directly on each questionnaire. For short polls, to cut costs and speed up analysis, answers may be recorded on answer sheets, or response sheets. Figure 4-2 gives an example of an answer sheet for the preceding questions.

 CHECKLIST FOR QUESTIONNAIRE CONSTRUCTION

1. Does each question solicit a specific piece of information that you need and do you know how you will use that information?
2. Have you decided what types of questions to use to solicit each piece of information?
3. Are your questions worded properly?
4. Are the response categories worded well, easy to remember, and comprehensive?
5. Does the questionnaire begin with an interesting, easy question and end with the demographics?
6. Are your questions grouped by topic, proceeding from general to specific?
7. Have you included instructions, directions, and probes for the interviewer?

INTERVIEW NO. _____

Q1. 1.1 INFLATION   1.6 TAXES
     1.2 JOBS   1.7 AGRICULTURE
     1.3 ENERGY   1.8 INTEREST RATES
     1.4 ENVIRONMENT   1.9 ECONOMY
     1.5 GOVT. SPENDING   1.10 OTHER
     1.98 DON'T KNOW   1.99–MISSING

Q2. 2.1 INFLATION   2.6 TAXES
     2.2 JOBS   2.7 AGRICULTURE
     2.3 ENERGY   2.8 INTEREST RATES
     2.4 ENVIRONMENT   2.9 ECONOMY
     2.5 GOVT. SPENDING   2.10 OTHER
     2.98 DON'T KNOW   2.99–MISSING

Q3.
     3.1 BETTER
     3.2 SAME
     3.3 WORSE
     3.98 DON'T KNOW
     3.99–MISSING

Q4.
     4.1 FAVOR
     4.2 OPPOSE
     4.98 DON'T KNOW
     4.99–MISSING

Q5. (for those who answered "FAVOR" above)
     5.1 YES
     5.2 NO
     5.98 DON'T KNOW
     5.99–MISSING OR NOT APPLICABLE

FIGURE 4–2 *Sample Answer Sheet for a Poll.*
(Circle answer)

8. Is the questionnaire easy to mark for the interviewer, with space for the answers to open-ended questions?
9. Has the layout of the questionnaire taken into consideration the needs of the coders and data entry people as well as the interviewers and respondents?

CHAPTER FIVE

Interviewing

This chapter discusses the polling interview, the principles behind successful interviewing, and some warnings and tips for success. Chapter 6 takes a closer look at recruiting and training interviewers and managing the pretest and the poll.

INTERVIEW AS SOCIAL INTERACTION OR "A LOOK AT A GOOD INTERVIEW"

The goal of any poll is to obtain the most accurate information possible. Because the interview is the vehicle for reaching that goal, it is one of the most important elements of any poll.

The interview should be neutral and not an attempt to influence opinion. This is more difficult than it sounds, however, because interviewing is actually a social interaction influenced by the goals and expectations of both the interviewer and respondent. For example, an interview closely resembles a test situation — respondents want to please the interviewer by appearing smart and giving the "correct" answers. The interviewer needs to "teach" the respondents how to answer correctly without suggesting what to answer.

A good interviewer should do the following:

- ☐ Communicate a commitment to the interview as an important, professional task. Interact with the respondent as if the commitment were mutual.
- ☐ Sound friendly and confident yet neutral and nondirective, interested and positive yet professional.

☐ Give respondents a clear idea of their role in the interview. Reward or reinforce good performance.

☐ Make sure respondents answer according to the categories provided using professional reinforcement and probing.

These guidelines are discussed in more detail later in this chapter.

THE "BURDEN" ON THE RESPONDENT AND THE REWARDS

Good interviewers understand that the interview places a burden on the respondent. The respondent will immediately try to figure out who is calling and what information is wanted. There are also costs to the respondent in an interviewing situation, such as:

☐ Commitment of time
☐ Inconvenience
☐ Mental work and the effort to retrieve information
☐ Infringement on privacy
☐ Possible embarrassment, boredom, and frustration with the topics

It is the interviewer's job quickly to legitimize the survey and convince the respondent that the rewards offset the costs of the interview. The rewards include:

☐ Interesting nature of the survey
☐ Interest the interviewer shows in the respondent's answers
☐ Importance of the respondent's answers to the quality of the poll
☐ Enjoyment in working out unique and interesting answers

Clear instructions, well-worded questions, well-timed interviews, and professional interviewing can all increase motivation and enjoyment of the interview experience.

BASIC PRINCIPLES OF INTERVIEWING— HOW DO I ASK QUESTIONS?

These next few sections examine key elements in the interview: asking the questions, establishing the pace, probing, reinforcement, and refusals.

Asking Questions

The following is a list of important guidelines to help you ask questions in a professional and neutral manner that will protect the quality of your poll:

☐ Read questions exactly as written without explanation, discussion, chitchat, or editorializing. If you're asked for an interpretation, say something like, "Whatever that means to you," or "I'm sorry, I have been instructed just to read the questions, and I really don't know the answer to that," or "Let me repeat the question for you." Recruiting interviewers who identify with the interest group conducting the survey rather than the topic itself will help reinforce these standards.

☐ Repeat the question and the response options if the respondent fails to give an answer among those options or gives more than one answer (unless the interview specifically calls for such).

☐ Remind respondents not to respond before you have read the entire question; they may change their minds after hearing the whole question if they answer too quickly.

☐ If you are unsure of a respondent's answer, repeat the answer and ask for confirmation.

☐ Don't guess which category is closest to an unclear response. Repeat the response categories and ask the respondent to choose. Say something like, "Yes, but is your answer X, Y, or Z?"

☐ Repeat the response options halfway through a long series of questions using the same scale. It is often not necessary to repeat the series after each question, but repeating halfway through may be helpful, especially if the respondent has given the same answer several times in a row. For example:

How do you feel about the job performance of these public agencies? Your choices are: "Very Positive," "Somewhat Positive," "Neutral," "Somewhat Negative," "Very Negative." Now I'll read a name, and you indicate which category best describes your feelings.

	VP	SP	N	SN	VN
Health Board					
Air Quality Board					
County Commission					
Mayor's Office					

☐ Do not omit any questions unless a "SKIP" pattern indicates that certain questions can be skipped because of answers to previous questions. Never change the sequence of questions. For example:

> Do you favor a general sales tax? POSSIBLE RESPONSES: "YES," "NO," "DON'T KNOW."
>
> IF THE ANSWER WERE "NO," ASK: Would you favor a sales tax if it meant property taxes would go down? RESPONSES: "YES," "NO," "DON'T KNOW," "MISSING," OR "NOT APPLICABLE."

☐ Do not fill in missed questions yourself. If questions are inadvertently skipped, leave them blank.

☐ Use voice intonation to emphasize endpoints of response options and any phrases underlined in the question. In telephone surveys, your voice is an important communication link, so use it to facilitate understanding of the questions and responses without suggesting one choice over another. For example:

> Generally speaking, do you feel you and your family are *better off* or *worse off* since the President took office?

 Important note: If interviewers and/or respondents are having trouble with a particular phrase or the interpretation of one particular question, bring it to the attention of your poll supervisor so a standard response can be developed. All respondents should receive the same stimuli.

Pace

Untrained interviewers usually read the interview too quickly. The proper pace is about two words per second, although the introduction may be read faster. Reading slowly gives the respondent time to think, communicates a sense of importance about the task, and provides time to reflect on a response once it is given.

 Important note: When recording the answer to an open-ended question (the respondent's words are taken down verbatim), be sure to tell the respondent what you are doing. Your respondent will wonder why the pace of the interview has slowed so much.

Probing

A probe is a follow-up question that stimulates correct answering or ends digressions as neutrally as possible. For example:

- ☐ "What did you mean by that answer?"
- ☐ "Could you be more specific about that?"
- ☐ "Anything else?"

Probes like these are used with open-ended questions to clarify and complete answers. Open-ended questions in particular need to be probed because respondents are never sure what or how much you want. For example:

> If you could change one thing in our state government, what would that be? _____ (TAKE DOWN ANSWERS VERBATIM.)

For close-ended questions (the response options are provided), probes are used when:

- ☐ An inadequate or incorrect answer has been given
- ☐ The only response is silence
- ☐ The respondent replies that he or she can't answer the question as asked (Moser and Kalton, 1974).

Reinforcement

Feedback, or reinforcement, is given in interviews to train people to behave in a certain way, that is, to respond fully to your questions to the best of their ability in terms of the categories you provide. Reinforcement should be neutral, consistent, and meaningful. It is particularly important in telephone surveys because interviewers cannot give any visual reinforcement to respondents.

Untrained interviewers most often give reinforcement to respondents after situations that are uncomfortable for the interviewer — for example, when the respondent has struggled with a question or given an inadequate response. Reinforcement at this time may send mixed signals by rewarding poor performance. It is important to assure respondents when they are having difficulty with a question, but it is also critical not to carry this assurance to the point of encouraging inadequate responses.

Performance, not content, should be rewarded. Reinforcement should be used when the respondent has actually performed the task well. Good performance involves answering questions with one of the responses offered, or for open-ended questions, answering with an original response that has some clarity and thoughtfulness.

Reinforcement should be general and neutral in nature. For example, you should say something like, "That is very helpful," or "That is just the type of information we need."

Clearly, the timing of your reinforcement is important. You don't want to give reinforcement just after your respondent has cast a favorable answer for your issue.

Refusals

Don't let a refusal to answer a specific question distress you or destroy the rapport you have built with a respondent. The most frequently refused questions involve demographic information such as income, age, voter registration, and sometimes political party affiliation. For this reason, these questions are usually placed at the end of the survey.

> Emphasize that these questions are for statistical purposes only and that the interview is strictly confidential. Be sure to accept a refusal in stride so that it does not cause the respondent to terminate the interview.

HOW DO I OBTAIN AN INTERVIEW?

Most interviewers think it is more difficult to get an interview than it actually is. People hear about polls all the time, and many individuals are pleased to have an opportunity to give their views to an interested listener.

Tips for Successful Interviews

In general, interview introductions should tell respondents that the interview is short and strictly confidential, that they have been chosen randomly, and that their views are important in your understanding of issues.

Success varies with the tone and skill of interviewers, the content of the introduction, how difficult the subject of the interview sounds, and the prestige or relevance of the poll's sponsor. During the introduction, a good interviewer's tone should be friendly, patient, professional, assertive, and sincere.

You should assume the respondent is willing to participate and never initiate the interview in a way that would make it easy for the respondent to say "No." For example, you should never say, "Do you want to continue?" or "May I continue?" If you sound like your arguments for doing the interview have been persuasive and use transitions like, "I'll start by asking you the first question," you will be more successful in engaging respondents.

Reasons for Refusals

There are several reasons why people refuse to be interviewed. They may not trust the interviewer, believing that the interviewer is really trying to sell something. They may not understand the task or feel that the poll is inconvenient or uninteresting. Refusal rates may be as high as 25% for surveys conducted by volunteers, although this rate can be lowered to 10-12% with refusal conversion. Refusal conversion is discussed later in this chapter. One third of refusals come within the first 10-15 seconds, the second third at the end of the second sentence of the introduction, and the last third when you ask to speak to the sampled individual (the "household/individual listing").

Important note: Don't accept a refusal too quickly from the respondent, and don't accept any substitute respondents or refusals by people other than the respondent chosen for your sample.

To get acceptable response rates, most surveys include making and following up on appointments made with people who were unavailable on the first call. Response rates and call-backs are discussed later in this chapter.

Partial Interviews

Partial interviews (interviews where the respondent quits in the middle) are more common in longer telephone surveys (usually over 15 minutes) and are especially prevalent in surveys lasting more than 40–45 minutes. Partial interviews can total 6–12% of the sample even in surveys done by professionals.

 A word of caution: Longer telephone surveys (20 minutes or longer) involve more work, more interviewing hours, and sometimes greater turnover and burnout of interviewers. Your organization should be aware of the additional work, frustration, and planning that longer surveys require.

Longer telephone surveys may necessitate arranging to interview the respondent on two different occasions. Try to keep these interviews as close to the same day as possible. Keep track of your appointments and where the interview should be resumed.

In many studies, a critical core of information is contained in the second half of the questionnaire. If a respondent wants to quit and refuses an appointment to resume the survey, the interviewer should try at least to get the answers to those critical questions. This should take not more than 5 minutes. Over half of these respondents can be convinced to answer "a few more basic questions."

If the respondent has answered the key questions, keep the interview, even though the rest will be considered "missing data."

Response Rates

A good telephone survey will have an overall response rate of 60–70%. This rate is calculated from the number of completed interviews (including partial interviews) divided by the number of names sampled (for samples drawn from lists of voters, for example) or the number of telephone numbers sampled (for samples drawn from telephone directories). The following is a list of general information about response rates:

☐ The quality and age of the list that you draw your sample from will affect the response rate of your survey. For example, voter registration lists that are over two years old will contain many names that cannot be reached.

☐ The response rates for telephone surveys will be slightly higher in urban areas than response rates for personal surveys.

☐ Your response rate may be slightly lower if you question many of the same people who were recently polled in a similar survey. Respondents will think they have already participated, may be fatigued and less interested, and also may have learned they can refuse to be interviewed.

☐ Response rates for samples of random telephone numbers are more difficult to calculate because of the high proportion of nonworking numbers in these samples. Calculating the response rate by taking the number of completed interviews divided by the number of working numbers will inflate the response rates for these types of samples.

Additional cautions are detailed in Chapter 7 on Sampling. For now, you should remember that any sampling design you develop should take into consideration these important factors affecting response rates for different types of surveys.

Refusal Conversion

It is usually necessary to do refusal conversions to obtain a good response rate. When an initial interviewer gets a refusal, detailed notes should be taken about the conversation and the respondent's questions and reservations. Toward the end of the study, the interviewers with the lowest refusal rates are assigned to refusal conversion. These conversion "experts" then call the respondents who refused, acknowledge that the respondents have been contacted before, emphasize the importance of the survey and the unique contribution respondents can make to the survey, and try to address the respondent's concerns and reservations.

Simply calling back often catches a respondent at a more convenient time or in a more receptive mood. You should remember, however, that this is stressful interviewing, even for the best interviewers. Supervisors should watch for signs of burnout in the individuals assigned to refusal conversion.

Despite its stressful nature, refusal conversion is a valuable tool and can lead to the completion of one third to one half of the original refusals. It is particularly successful when the original interviewing was done by volunteers because interviewing skill varies widely, and response rates are lower with volunteer interviewers than with professionals. Refusal conversion calls should be scheduled at least four days after the original call. Such calls should also be made, if possible, at a different time than the original call.

HOW DO I INTRODUCE THE SURVEY?

The interviewer's tone and confidence are more important than the content of the introduction in establishing an initial communication link with the respondent in the first 10–15 seconds. Refusals occur so quickly in telephone interviews that it is crucial for the introduction to allay fears quickly and establish the positive value of the survey. Because this is hard to do verbally, refusals come even sooner in telephone surveys than in personal interviews. It is rare, however, for respondents to hang up without giving a reason for refusing.

Introduction to the Survey

The introduction to the survey should be standardized and printed on the questionnaire or coversheet. Standard responses to frequently asked questions should be included in the interviewer's materials. A typical introduction tells who is calling, who you represent, and why you are calling. The topic of the survey should be introduced in such a way that you interest the respondent, keep the study description general enough so that respondents feel they know something about the topic, avoid creating expectations in the respondents' minds about what answers you want, and protect the sound of the study's neutrality.

Follow-up statements usually include information about the confidentiality of responses, a statement about the shortness of the survey or a statement about the option to make an appointment if the survey is long, information about the importance of the respondent's participation, and perhaps information about how the respondent's name was selected.

Here is a sample introduction with appropriate follow-ups:

> Hello, my name is _____. I'm calling for Montana Opinion Research, an independent public opinion organization. We are doing a survey in Montana about the issues and problems facing this state. You have been scientifically selected to be in this study. We would like to ask you a few short questions. (PAUSE)
>
> This interview only takes about 20 minutes. I can do the interview now or set up an appointment to interview you at your convenience. (PAUSE)
>
> Before we start, I want to assure you that your answers will be kept in strictest confidence. If we come to a question you would prefer not to answer, just let me know and we will go on to the next question.

CALL-BACKS

If you do not get an answer or otherwise cannot reach the respondent on the first call, you should use a call-back procedure to ensure a valid sample for your survey. This means calling the respondent back at different times on different days.

Most good surveys use at least three call-backs, which means calling back three times on three different days at three different times during the day. This is an attempt to reach the respondent before going on to a replacement or dropping the listing. Three call-backs (thus a total of four calls) are used because it is a feasible number of calls to make and because experience has shown over 80% of the people you would ever be able to reach can be reached in four calls. Figure 6-1 in the next chapter shows an example of a coversheet needed to keep track of appointments and call-backs.

In most studies you interview about 30% of respondents on the first call, 30% on the second call, about 20% on the third call, and about 10% on the fourth call. Interviewers should be trained to let the phone ring five times before hanging up.

Sometimes it is difficult to tell whether a number is working if no one ever answers. The central telephone office for the area often can verify whether the number is a working number.

If a number is busy, you should call back in half an hour. You may ultimately do more than three call-backs if a number is busy, or if you have made appointments.

Appointments

Try to make appointments or find another good time to call the respondent if someone else answers the call. You should not do the interview with just anyone who answers, even if the respondent is unavailable.

Neglecting to do call-backs or interviewing whoever answers the telephone seriously biases the results of a survey. These shortcomings cause systematic oversampling of certain kinds of people (usually women and senior citizens) and systematic undersampling of others (blue-collar workers, young people, and mobile people). The danger of this serious bias to the quality of your poll is reason enough to make and keep appointments with respondents.

Several other factors affect your ability to make and complete your appointments. The most important factor is that response rates for different kinds of people will vary by day of the week and time of the day. For example, you will get fewer men on Monday nights, more women around mealtimes, more employed couples on weekends, and so on. The best time to call may vary with the population sampled and characteristics of the region (for example, local activities and shift changes). These all need to be considered when planning your survey and strategizing appointments.

The next chapter explores in more detail who should do your interviews, how they should be trained, and how you should manage and administer your poll. The checklists for this chapter and Chapter 6 have been consolidated and presented at the end of Chapter 6.

CHAPTER SIX

Preparing for and Managing Your Interviews

This chapter follows up on the interviewing information detailed in the previous chapter. We'll discuss recruitment and training of interviewers and give tips for successful managing of the interviewing segment of your poll.

WHO SHOULD DO THE INTERVIEWING?

Recruitment

The first step in good interviewing is recruiting people with the following basic interviewing abilities:

- ☐ Friendliness and an outgoing personality
- ☐ Persistence, care, and attention to details
- ☐ Ability to follow instructions
- ☐ A schedule that allows them to call at night and on weekends
- ☐ Good reading skills and a pleasant voice without an obvious accent different from your region's accent. (In Spanish-speaking areas you will need some Spanish-speaking interviewers, of course.)

 Important note: Not all people with these abilities, however, will turn out to be good interviewers. You should monitor your interviewers' initial response rates (particularly their refusal rates) and edit their initial interviews. Do not hesitate to replace interviewers who are not successful in obtaining interviews or who are not doing a good job for you.

One other caution: Interest groups often recruit volunteer interviewers who have been telephone solicitors. This is not always a good choice. Solicitation is quite different from surveying, and such callers often have trouble adopting a neutral, nondirective style.

You will save yourself a lot of headaches if you recruit enough interviewers at the beginning to finish your tasks and get a firm schedule of interviewers on paper before you begin the poll. Here are some guidelines to help you determine how many interviewers you will need:

- ☐ No interviewer should do more than 20% of the interviews. This should help reduce "interviewer bias" — the effect of deviations in responses due to the subtle influences of the interviewer.
- ☐ Try to keep a core of good interviewers throughout the project. Large groups with a high turnover rate are hard to motivate and monitor.
- ☐ Anticipate turnover and burnout rates even with your best interviewers if you are working with volunteers.
- ☐ Be realistic about the task you are doing, how long it will take, and how important it is to your organization. Be sure to communicate that realistic assessment to your interviewers.

Professionals Versus Volunteers

There are obvious tradeoffs for an organization between hiring (and paying) trained professional interviewers and recruiting volunteers. Professional interviewers tend to complete more interviews per hour, have a higher response rate, and introduce less interviewer bias and error into your survey. Professional interviewers also tend to have a lower turnover and burnout rate. Their sense of professionalism and responsibility for the survey contributes to the quality of your poll. They also cost money.

Volunteers can be very successful as interviewers, but they must be well-trained, reinforced, monitored, and given a well-organized task. Unless volunteers "own" a sense of professionalism and responsibility for the survey, high turnover rates and poor results can plague your poll.

Don't forget: There will be some difficult decisions to make about your interviewers. Your initial core of interviewers should be evaluated after the first few sessions, and poor interviewers should be moved to other jobs. Good, conscientious, popular volunteers may still turn out to be poor interviewers. As a supervisor, you should be prepared to deal with that possibility quickly and effectively.

HOW DO I TRAIN MY INTERVIEWERS?

Elements of Training Sessions

Thorough training is essential if you are to neutralize and standardize interviewer behavior. In addition, the ability of good training to motivate your volunteers cannot be underestimated. Allow an hour to an hour and a half for the initial training of your core interviewers. Then pull aside new interviewers each night for about 20 minutes of training. Send out a packet beforehand if possible with the questionnaire and tips for interviewing. Be sure to include adequate role playing in the training.

A good training session begins with:

- ☐ A discussion of the purpose of the poll and how the sample was drawn.
- ☐ A clear discussion of the goals of the survey.
- ☐ Detailed instruction on the processes to be used in interviewing.
- ☐ Reminders to remain neutral and nondirective to avoid influencing respondents' answers.

It may be particularly important for you to remind your interviewers (especially if they are volunteers) that they should not worry about the trends they may see in the responses to their interviews. First, the number of calls any one interviewer makes is too small to accurately support any valid conclusions. Second, even if the news is bad, the point of the poll is to find out the good and the bad before it is too late to act on the information.

Sampling

When you discuss the sample, you will need to go over:

☐ How to use the coversheet correctly
☐ How to choose the respondents correctly
☐ How to do household listings
☐ When to use alternates
☐ How to do. any initial screening, when applicable
☐ Procedures for special situations. For example, no
   interviewer should call anyone they know personally (their
   name should be given to another interviewer)

These techniques are discussed in detail in Chapter 7 on Sampling.

Interviewing

Next you should discuss the basic principles of interviewing,
including:

☐ Probing and reinforcement
☐ Answers to commonly asked questions
☐ Introduction to the questionnaire
☐ How to obtain an interview

Interviewers frequently are given a sheet or card with reminders
of good interviewing techniques that can be posted near their telephone station. Figure 6-1 is an example of such a card:

REMINDERS FOR INTERVIEWING

✔ BE FRIENDLY AND INTERESTED . . . SO PEOPLE WANT TO
TALK WITH YOU.

✔ BE PROFESSIONAL . . . USE REINFORCEMENT AND PROBING
TO GET FULL ANSWERS AND TO MOTIVATE RESPONDENTS TO
DO THE BEST JOB.

✔ BE POSITIVE . . . ASSUME THE RESPONDENT IS WILLING TO
BE INTERVIEWED.

✔ BE PATIENT BUT ASSERTIVE . . . SET UP AN APPOINTMENT IF
THIS IS A BAD TIME AND EMPHASIZE THE IMPORTANCE OF
GETTING THE RESPONDENT'S PARTICIPATION.

✔ BE NEUTRAL . . . DO NOT INFLUENCE ANSWERS, CHITCHAT,
OR HELP WITH ANSWERS.

FIGURE 6-1

✔ BE EXACT . . . READ EACH QUESTION EXACTLY AS WRITTEN.

✔ BE ACCURATE . . . RECORD THE RESPONSE AND FOLLOW INSTRUCTIONS CORRECTLY.

✔ BE POLITE . . . MAKE THE INTERVIEW A PLEASANT EXPERIENCE FOR THE RESPONDENT.

FIGURE 6-1 *(continued)*

Recording and Editing Answers

Training concerning recording and editing answers should include:

☐ How to record answers correctly (either with an "X" or by circling the correct responses).

☐ How to edit the questionnaire after the call is done — spelling out abbreviations, precoding, and notes; filling in the missing data codes for missed questions or questions correctly skipped in a "skip pattern."

☐ How to use the answer sheet or how to mark the questionnaire directly if no answer sheet is used.

☐ Instructions on legible writing, use of pencils, and other logistics.

☐ Special instructions on recording open-ended questions.

☐ Completion by interviewers of questions that can be answered without asking the respondent (such as sex and county).

In most cases, interviewers will be able to mark answers right on the questionnaire by circling or marking the number of the response. Usually only one response per question should be marked, and it should be a category specifically given by the respondent.

Most questions will have a "Don't Know" option. This response should be marked if the respondent actually says he or she is undecided. It should not be read unless it is explicitly in the question wording. If a respondent changes an answer, interviewers should mark a slash through the first mark and mark the new answer.

 Instructions to interviewers are typically typed in capital letters and in parentheses (LIKE THIS, for example). Complicated skip pattern instructions should be boxed off for special notice. When reading the poll, interviewers should read only the printed question unless specifically instructed otherwise. For example:

Q1. Would you *favor* or *oppose* giving parents of parochial school children a break in their income tax for this tuition?

    ○ 1.1 FAVOR→GO TO Q2
    ○ 1.2 OPPOSE—(SKIP TO Q3)
    ○ 1.3 DON'T KNOW (SKIP TO Q3)
    ○ 1.99 MISSING (INCLUDING NOT ASCERTAINED)

Q2. Would you favor an income tax break for parents of parochial school children even if it reduced the amount of money available for public schools?

    ○ 2.1 YES
    ○ 2.2 NO
    ○ 2.3 DON'T KNOW
    ○ 2.9 MISSING (INCLUDING CORRECTLY SKIPPED)

Open-ended questions present you with special problems for recording answers. Pay extra attention to these questions. Answers to open-ended questions should be recorded completely and exactly as given by the respondent. A helpful guideline is that the recorded answer should be clear to a third reader as well as to the interviewer. For example:

Q. What do you personally feel is the most important problem currently facing our state? Anything else?

First mention: *"The drug problem of our young people"* _____

Second mention: *"The high cost of utilities and no place to get help"*

If something is unclear, the interviewer should say, "What do you mean by this?" Don't worry about badgering; most respondents will be pleased that you are paying such close attention. Encourage respondents for full answers by using such phrases as, "Anything else?" after the first response.

If a respondent is talking too fast, interviewers can slow things down by repeating the answer as they write. This will communicate a subtle message to the respondents that their answers are being written down and they need to go slower.

Procedures

In this portion of training, you should go over the procedures, or logistics, of your poll:

☐ What the schedule is for calling
☐ Where interviewers get materials — pencils, coversheets, instructions, interviews — when they arrive
☐ Where you have posted the reminder sheets of basic interviewing procedures
☐ Where to put finished interviews, refusals, appointments, nonworking numbers, and other problem cases.

If you have a high turnover rate among your volunteers, you will want to train people frequently throughout the interviewing. An initial training session for all volunteers is important if basic procedures are to be followed and your survey is to go as smoothly as possible.

Q by Q—Question by Question

Once the procedures have been learned, you're ready to take your interviewers through the questionnaire — question by question:

☐ Read through each question, emphasizing any instructions or skip patterns.
☐ Provide additional clarification for questions that require more than the simple instruction printed with the question (see Figure 6-2).
☐ Discuss the separate sheet of "Q by Qs" that alert interviewers to special problems inherent in certain questions.
☐ Be sure to alert interviewers to questions that may be asked differently depending on where they are calling. For example, a statewide poll may have a congressional race question that would require the substitution of the appropriate candidates in the districts.

Figure 6-2 gives examples of two questions that warrant further instructions: a most important problem question (often taken down as an open-ended question and then precoded by interviewers) and a thermometer question.

Most Important Problem Question

1. What do you feel is the most important problem facing Montana? (Anything else?)

First mention: _____

Second mention: _____

    ○ 01. INFLATION
    ○ 02. JOBS & UNEMPLOYMENT
    ○ 03. ENERGY
    ○ 04. GOVERNMENT SPENDING
    ○ 05. TAXES
    ○ 06. AGRICULTURE (FARMS & PRICES)
    ○ 07. OTHER
    ○ 98. DON'T KNOW
    ○ 99. NO SECOND MENTION (USE ON SECOND MENTION ONLY), MISSING

Sample of further instructions

"THIS IS THE ONLY QUESTION WHERE YOU WRITE OUT THE ENTIRE ANSWER *AND* CODE IT YOURSELF. YOU SHOULD FIT THE RESPONDENT'S ANSWER INTO ONE OF THE CODE CATE-GORIES AS CLEARLY AS POSSIBLE, USING THE "OTHER" CATEGORY AS A LAST RESORT. *DO NOT READ* THE CODE CATEGORIES TO RESPONDENTS."

THERMOMETER QUESTION

Now I'd like to get your feelings toward some groups in Montana. You will rate these groups on something we call the "Feeling Thermometer," and here is how it works: I'll read the name of a group, and then ask you to rate that group using a thermometer which runs from 0 degrees (very cool) to 100 degrees (very warm). On this thermometer, ratings between 50 and 100 degrees mean that you feel favorable and warm toward that group. Ratings between 0 and 50 degrees mean that you don't feel too favorable toward that group. If you don't feel particularly warm or cool, you would rate it at 50 degrees (neutral). If you don't know the group, just tell me and we'll move on to the next group. Now, on this scale, which runs from 0 degrees (very cool) to 100 degrees (very warm), how would you rate your feelings toward:

FIGURE 6–2 *Example of a "Q by Q."*

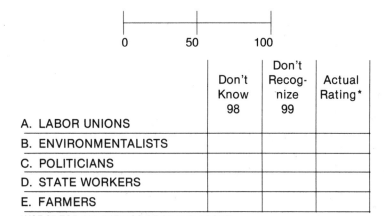

	Don't Know 98	Don't Recog- nize 99	Actual Rating*
A. LABOR UNIONS			
B. ENVIRONMENTALISTS			
C. POLITICIANS			
D. STATE WORKERS			
E. FARMERS			

*USE 97 FOR ALL RATINGS OF 97 AND ABOVE.

Sample of further instructions:

READ THE INSTRUCTIONS AND MAKE SURE YOU UNDER-
STAND HOW THIS QUESTION WORKS BEFORE YOU BEGIN
INTERVIEWING. FOUR CODES THAT YOU SHOULD BE
ESPECIALLY AWARE OF ARE "99," TO BE USED WHEN THE
RESPONDENT DOES NOT RECOGNIZE THE GROUP, "98," TO
BE USED WHEN THE RESPONDENT RECOGNIZES THE
GROUP BUT DOES NOT KNOW WHERE TO RATE IT, "50,"
WHICH YOU ARE TO USE IF THE RESPONDENT FEELS NEU-
TRAL ABOUT THE GROUP, AND "97" FOR RATINGS OF 97
AND HIGHER. BE SURE THE RESPONDENT UNDERSTANDS
THIS IS A FULL SCALE WHERE THEY CAN USE ANY VALUE
FROM 0 TO 100, NOT JUST THOSE VALUES SPECIFICALLY
MENTIONED BY YOU.

FIGURE 6-2 *(continued)*

Role Playing

Probably the most important part of training is role playing, in
which trainees:

1. Watch an experienced person conduct an interview.
2. Role play with one or more of each other.
3. Call someone they do not know who is not in the sample.

For telephone interviewing, the mock interview should not be
face-to-face because telephone interviewing is quite different from
personal interviewing.

Role playing should particularly cover open-ended questions and probing, how to get an interview, and nondirective reinforcement. It is the most important part of the training and may also help you spot poor interviewers early. You will want to review several different situations in the role playing, such as a wordy respondent and a reluctant one.

Dealing With Frequently Asked Questions

The following is a list of some questions that are asked frequently of interviewers:

- ☐ Who is doing this research?
- ☐ How did you get my number?
- ☐ How will this be used?
- ☐ Is this a political survey?
- ☐ Why don't you interview my husband/wife instead?
- ☐ Why do you need to know the persons in my household?

Your answers to these questions should be standard, printed for each interviewer, and as honest, reassuring, and nondirective as possible. Your training should include a review of your answers to these anticipated questions.

Wrap-Up

You should end your training by answering any final questions. Then give one of the most important ingredients: the pep talk, in which you recognize that all of this may be overwhelming, especially to volunteers. Motivation is particularly important to promote good interviewing and minimize burnout and turnover among your volunteers. To keep your volunteers motivated, you might consider posting how many interviews have been completed, keeping it updated or promising to send interviewers a summary of the results to increase their feeling of "belonging" to the inner circle of the poll. Confidentiality of your poll may necessitate withholding some information, but do find some things you can share. A good talk will include a review of the goals of the survey and how the information will be used. Remind interviewers that most respondents will enjoy the experience and will not feel imposed upon.

MONITORING — KEEPING INTERVIEWERS ON TRACK

As critical as good training is in reducing error and bias in your survey, the quality of interviewing will deteriorate if interviewers are not monitored. Monitoring is especially important in the beginning to pick up errors. When monitoring:

- ☐ Listen while interviewers make calls.
- ☐ Check that questionnaires are edited and filled out correctly.
- ☐ Make sure the sample is being used correctly.
- ☐ Check interviewers' response and refusal rates.
- ☐ Give feedback on interviewers' performance, especially in the beginning. This stresses the professionalism of the task and corrects poor procedures early.
- ☐ Maintain two-way communication throughout the poll to receive information on questions and procedures that are not working.

Don't forget that your interviewers are human beings, and while you monitor their performance, make sure you also monitor their motivation needs. An "on-the-spot" pep talk can be very helpful, especially with volunteers.

HOW TO TEST THE QUESTIONNAIRE AND PROCEDURES

The Pretest

Don't commit one of the worst, but most common, mistakes in surveying: neglecting to pretest your questionnaire. You cannot change the questionnaire halfway through the poll without affecting the validity of your poll.

Important note: There is no substitute for interviewing to test your question wording, question order, procedures, and interviewer instructions.

In the pretest, you interview people as similar as possible to your sample population to see how your questionnaire is working. By so doing, you can make revisions to avoid problems and makeshift solutions after the survey has started.

To conduct a pretest:

☐ Draw a small sample (20–30 individuals from several areas) of people who are similar to but not part of your sample.

☐ Use well-trained interviewers, preferably some experienced and some new volunteers, to interview respondents.

☐ Interviewers should take careful notes on respondents' reactions as well as their answers to questions.

☐ Have interviewers verify that all instructions and "skip" patterns are correct.

☐ Have interviewers ask respondents for their general reactions to the questionnaire at the end of the interview.

☐ Interviewers then get together and go over the questionnaire item by item, noting questions that worked and those that need revision.

☐ Watch for questions that are awkward to read, unclear, do not provide answer categories respondents want to use, seem repetitious, are influenced by earlier questions, or are hard for respondents to remember. Watch for no variance in your answers because all respondents say the same thing or have no opinion. These problems suggest that questions need to be reworded.

Figure 6-3 presents a sample pretest form that interviewers can use to evaluate a questionnaire. It gives you and your interviewers an idea of what to watch for in a pretest. (Additional alerts are presented in Chapter 3 on Questionnaire Wording and Construction.)

DON'T FORGET ABOUT SUPERVISING THE SURVEY

It should be obvious by now that with different shifts of interviewers, call-backs, appointments, and sampling procedures, the interviewing phase of a survey requires major planning and supervision. Remember that interviewers actually spend only one-half to two-thirds of their time interviewing, which indicates the importance of the other tasks they perform.

 You will need one supervisor for every 10–20 telephones if you are using a centralized location. You will need more supervisors in the beginning when you are monitoring

Length

1. How long did the interviews take? (Record the length of each interview)

Administrative ease

1. Were any questions difficult to read? (List the question and the difficult phrase)
2. Once you were familiar with the questionnaire, were there any parts where "skip" patterns were confusing or you didn't know how to mark the question? (List the question and the problem)
3. Did you have enough room to record responses? (List the problems)

Respondent's Understanding of Questionnaire

1. Were there any questions you had to repeat to the respondent? (List)
2. Were there any questions you felt the respondent misunderstood? (Which ones? What was the nature of the misunderstanding?)
3. Were there any questions the respondent thought were asking the same thing as other questions? Did respondents ever refer to answers of previous questions in answering later ones? (List the pairs)
4. Were there any questions for which you had to repeat the response categories because the respondent couldn't remember the categories or didn't understand them? (Which ones and what were the problems?)
5. Were there any questions where respondents wanted to respond using categories other than those we offered them, or where people wanted to qualify their responses? (Which questions and how did they want to respond?)
6. Were there any questions or response categories that were offensive or to which respondents objected? (Which and what problems?)
7. What questions did the respondent ask you during the interview? (List the questions and the place in the interview where they occurred)

General evaluation

1. What was the respondent's reaction, if any, to the questionnaire? (Include remarks from your debriefing)
2. As an interviewer, what was your reaction to the questionnaire?
3. In general, how would you describe the interview and the respondent? (List for each interview)

FIGURE 6-3 *A Sample Pretest Form for Evaluation of a Questionnaire*

interviewers, training new interviewers every night, and calling to recruit and remind volunteers. You should provide separate training for the supervisors.

The person in charge of the survey needs to lay out a plan early so that interviewers, available telephones, supervisors, questionnaires, sample listings, and interviewer materials are all ready to go at the same time. After volunteers are trained and set to interview, everything should be ready to start immediately. Interviewing time and volunteers' time are too precious to waste.

One note of caution: Some parts of a survey regularly take more time and work than initially estimated. From our experience, these parts commonly include recruiting enough interviewers and replacements when needed, securing the lists for and preparing the sample, and nightly training of interviewers. It is wise to build some extra time for these tasks into your plan.

HOW DO I KEEP TRACK OF THE SAMPLE AND INTERVIEWS?

Coversheet

Every sample listing, including telephone number, voter name, telephone directory listing, and so forth, should be assigned to a **coversheet.** The coversheet:

☐ Allows you to keep track of the sample, the result of each call, and appointments all at the same time.

☐ Contains a place for the sample listing, the interviewer's name, a record of calls, and an interview number.

☐ May contain the introduction and additional sampling information to make the interviewer's job easier.

☐ Be as complete as possible, giving a name and address for the primary sample name, as well as names and addresses of replacements if you are using this method.

☐ Has enough room to write in telephone numbers once they are looked up and room for notes and extra comments.

Figure 6-4 presents a sample coversheet.

Sample label   Interview No. _____
                                Interviewer name _____

Hello, my name is _____. I am calling from the Montana Opinion Poll . . .

Call record:

Call:	Date	Time	Result of call	Appointment date/time
1				
call-back 1				
call-back 2				
call-back 3				

Refusal: please, explain _____

_____

_____

Appointment: additional information _____

FIGURE 6-4 *Sample coversheet*

Call Results

Interviewers should record the result of each call on the coversheet: date, time, and result code. If an appointment is made, this should be indicated. The supervisor should develop procedures for keeping track of appointments for each shift and assigning them to interviewers.

 Important note: There is also room on the coversheet to elaborate on who in the household made the appointment, if the call-back is to complete a partial interview, and if so where to begin, and the reasons for or circumstances surrounding a refusal. This helps those who are doing refusal conversions to know where and how to start.

The following is a list of common abbreviations used in recording the results of calls:

INT   Interview completed
REF   Refusal

PART   Partial interview and no appointment to continue

APPT   Appointment (note the time and date. If you are calling across time zones, note the interviewer's and respondent's local times)

BZ   Busy

DIS   Disconnected

NA   Rang, but no answer

NW   Number not working

NONRES   Nonresidential number

DEC   Respondent deceased

NOLIS   No telephone listing available

The last two codes are only used when calling from lists of individuals. A list of result codes should be posted near each telephone.

Once an interview is completed, the supervisor should assign an interview number to the coversheet and to the first page of the interview. (With the POLLSTART software designed to complement this package, this is limited to a four-digit number.) That number also will be used in the data set and ultimately will be a link among your data set, your sample, and your interview.

HOW MUCH TIME WILL INTERVIEWING TAKE?

The amount of time the interviewing will take depends on the nature of the sample, length of the questionnaire, number of volunteers, and number of telephones available.

 Important note: Ideally, you don't want to conduct the calling part of a survey for more than two weeks. Things may happen during the interviewing period that will influence the results of your survey, so you should conduct your interviewing as quickly as possible. For example, a natural catastrophe may occur in the middle of your survey on local government services, or your opponent may be caught in a scandal in the middle of your political poll.

On the other hand, you need to allow enough days for your volunteers to make three call-backs, do refusal conversions, and do some calling on weekends to reach busy respondents. It is difficult to do a survey of any magnitude in less than five days.

When to Call

Calling is usually done:

☐ From 5 to 9:30 P.M. Monday through Thursday
☐ From 9 A.M. to 4 P.M. on Saturday
☐ From 12 to 9:30 P.M. on Sunday

So few people are home or willing to be interviewed on Friday and Saturday evenings and Sunday mornings that usually it is not worth calling at these times. With most samples, not enough people are home to make calling worthwhile during the day. However, you will need to have at least one daytime interviewer available for appointments and for respondents who are never home at night or on weekends.

Planning

First, you need to time how long it takes to read the questionnaire. Then, keeping in mind how large your sample is, you will be able to calculate the number of interviewers and telephones you will need and how many days you will have to call. With volunteers, you should allow 10-20 additional minutes per respondent to get the interview and determine the respondent. (All this varies with the nature of the sample list, whether household listings must be done, and whether call-backs and appointments are made.)

The following case study in poll planning should give you an idea of the kinds of resources you will need. Here are the specifics:

☐ Needed: completed surveys from a sample of 400 registered voters.
☐ Fifteen-minute questionnaire.
☐ Five telephones in use in the telephone bank.
☐ Calculated on the above information, interviewers should be scheduled on telephones for 33.5 hours.

This calculation is reached by estimating conservatively that you'll be able to complete two to three interviews an hour per telephone. You should use a conservative estimate to take into consideration time lost in refusals, busy signals, making appointments, and so on.

Therefore, instead of estimating that you'll complete four of the 15-minute interviews within an hour (that is, 20 interviews per telephone bank of five phones), you should estimate two to three interviews per telephone, or 12 interviews per telephone bank. Dividing the goal of 400 completed interviews by 12 gives you the number of hours required, or about 33.5 hours of telephone bank operation.

You could expect to finish this study with three call-backs and refusal conversion in no less than ten days. The study could take longer if you had to look up telephone numbers, do household listings, or if you had inadequately trained interviewers. Your schedule might look like this:

- ☐ Eight shifts — one each night (Monday–Thursday) and two each on Saturday and Sunday.
- ☐ Interviewers working at least two or three entire shifts per week.
- ☐ A total of 25 interviewers at three shifts per week.
- ☐ A couple of extra interviewers for a few days to finish required call-backs and do refusal conversions.

There's no question that interviewing with volunteers takes longer than with professionals. It's a vicious cycle, however, because the longer the interviewing period, the higher the turnover of volunteers and the longer the study is extended.

Important note: As questionnaire length increases, interviewing is also extended disproportionately because interviewers are forced to make more appointments and call-backs to finish partial interviews.

WHAT ABOUT HAVING PEOPLE CALL FROM HOME?

Centralized Interviewing

Finding a centralized telephone bank is one of the most difficult tasks for public interest groups, yet it is one of the most critical if you plan to use volunteers to conduct the interviews. Centralized telephoning makes it easier to:

☐ Keep track of interviews
☐ Spot errors
☐ Answer questions and solve problems
☐ Continue training
☐ Monitor interviewer performance
☐ Maintain high interviewing quality

You are more likely to finish your survey if you can interview in several central locations. Good places for multiple telephone lines are construction firms, law offices, your own offices, union headquarters, banks, and the like. If you have a choice, pick areas where interviewers will want to come at night and places that have push-button telephones.

Important note: Be sure your interviewers are seated far enough apart so that others' conversations are not distracting. If people must sit close to one another, "telephoning booths" can be constructed with two large sheets of cardboard on either side of the interviewer to act as a noise screen.

If you are forced to send interviews home with volunteers, be sure to provide for close supervision. You also may want to have your supervisors verify some of the interviews by recontacting a portion of the sample, repeating a couple of the factual questions, and asking respondents if they remembered the interview. Actually, not all respondents will remember being interviewed nor respond the same, but this is a partial check to make sure that volunteers are not fabricating interviews.

BEFORE YOU SAY GOODBYE, REMEMBER INTERVIEWER ETHICS

All of your interviewers should remember basic survey ethics. Respondents are guaranteed confidentiality, and their responses should not be discussed or presented in any way that can identify them without their prior consent. Interviewers should be honest in their interviewing. They should not make up answers to questions they have skipped or replace survey respondents with friends or other people. Likewise, supervisors should give interviewers reasonable tasks with reasonable time constraints so that interviewers are not forced to resort to dishonest shortcuts to meet deadlines.

✓ | CHECKLIST—INTERVIEWING

1. Have you calculated how much interviewing time you need?
2. Have you recruited enough interviewers, including a few extra for a few days?
3. Have you found centralized telephone banks?
4. Have you set up a training meeting?
5. Did you prepare an introduction for the survey?
6. Have you prepared coversheets and transferred the sample list to the coversheets?
7. Have you set up procedures for refusal conversions?
8. Have you set up procedures for monitoring and checking the interviewers?
9. Have you assembled the interviewer training materials, including basic instructions, question guides, and so on?
10. Have you set up an adequate system to handle appointments and call-backs?

CHAPTER SEVEN

Sampling

WHAT ARE THE BASIC PRINCIPLES OF SAMPLING?

What is an Unbiased Sample?

Selecting the sample is one of the most scientific aspects of polling. It must be done precisely, correctly, and in an unbiased manner. In sampling, **bias** has a very specific meaning: the systematic over- or underrepresentation of certain kinds of people.

To ensure an unbiased survey, you want your sample to have randomness. This means, for example, in a survey of teachers in Wyoming that every possible teacher in that state has an equal probability or chance of being selected as a respondent in your poll, and subsequently of being interviewed by you.

The Goal of Sampling

The goal of a sample is the accurate representation of the opinions of a group of people without really talking to every member of that group. To choose a sample, you would choose a small subset of people (i.e., the **sample**) from the larger group that interests you (i.e., the **population**). After interviewing the subset, you will know, with a known degree of confidence or certainty, the opinions of the larger group.

With the sample, you will have a known rate of error that comes from the size of your sample and the technique you used to draw it, which is called your sampling error within a certain **confidence interval.** Thus, you will be able to say that 95% of the time the real percentage response that you would get to any question if you inter-viewed the entire population is between x% and y%. The sizes of "x" and "y" depend on the sampling error. For example, a sample of 500 teachers may show that 64% want to go on strike. Actually, the real views, if you talked to all of the teachers, would be 60% to 68% — i.e., the sampling error is ± 45%.

Important note: No amount of care in interviewing and analysis can remove the bias inherent in a bad sample. Unlike other forms of error introduced in polls, sampling error that comes from poor sampling techniques usually biases your results in one direction or another rather than cancelling itself out.

Before drawing the sample, it is important to:

- ☐ Thoroughly understand the basic principles of sampling to reduce error and frustration later.
- ☐ Not underestimate the magnitude of the task you are undertaking and the time involved.
- ☐ Consider asking for professional help in approving and supervising your sampling procedures.

Definitions

Sampling is a systematic selection procedure and in most cases requires obtaining a list (called the **sampling frame**) which covers the population. The procedure involves choosing a random starting point and selecting subsequent respondents at a **fixed interval** from that point. This is the easiest form of simple random sampling, and the quality of the sample usually depends on how accurately the list covers the population. This chapter discusses other forms of sampling used in telephone interviewing, which are really variants of this simple technique, and describes in more detail this type of sampling.

Reading Surveys

As a consumer of surveys, always look at the end of any report or article for a description of the sampling pro-cedures used. This chapter should help you evaluate how good other studies' samples are as well as your own samples. Sampling is the most important thing you can evaluate as a consumer of polls.

Any description of a sample should give the dates of the interview, mode of the interview, sample size, error margin, the **confidence interval** on which that error is calculated (usually 95%), and an indication of the sampled population. Always include such a description in public releases of information about your own surveys.

THE SAMPLING FRAME

Definition

The sampling frame is the list from which you pull your sample. First you have to identify the population that interests you: whose attitudes do you want to generalize about or describe? Populations usually are described by some geographic, social, or political characteristic — for example, all Hispanic persons (social), all voters (political), all Coloradans (geographic).

Part of determining the population is figuring out beforehand how to measure certain characteristics. For example, how do you plan to measure voters: will you use the list of all registered voters, all people who voted at the last election, all citizens over 18 years of age, or what?

Choosing the wrong sampling frame can irreparably damage your survey and prove very misleading in your interpretation. For example, you would never want to draw conclusions about how parents of young children feel about public education by sampling all citizens over 18 years of age.

An important point to remember in defining the population is to be as clear and specific as possible. You must be able to tell easily whether a potential respondent is in your population or not.

Sample Unit

Once you have figured out how to describe the population you want to sample, you need to define the unit you are interested in interviewing: is it a household, individual, organization, or what?

In most opinion surveys (telephone or personal), we really think of interviewing households, which means we would not interview more than one person at a given address or telephone number. This procedure turns out to be representative, less contaminating, and easier to administer than techniques that actually sample individuals. Of course, even though you are sampling households, you actually are interviewing individuals within those households.

List of the Population

Once you have defined your population, you ideally want to get a list that gives you the name and telephone number and/or address of every person in the relevant population. In telephone polls of political subjects, we usually use one of four types of lists: lists of registered voters; telephone directories; crisscross, reverse, or street directories; or lists of telephone numbers (usually generated randomly by computer).

Registered Voters

Lists of registered voters are the easiest to use because the list can be limited easily to only those people who are geographically in the district or state. These lists also limit the sample to the relevant population for political surveys. Organizations often are not interested in the opinions of everyone in the district, but rather in the opinions of eligible voters, who are therefore decision makers on public policy matters.

Even for political surveys, however, lists of registered voters can be poor sampling frames if they do not include a large segment of people who would actually be eligible to vote in the election. Thus, they would be poor sampling frames if you expect a large registration drive to take place after your survey is taken.

Directories

Crisscross directories, where available, are useful for all types of surveys. Like lists of registered voters, they can be limited easily to the geographic boundaries of a district, state, town, and so on. Crisscross directories list telephone numbers and names by address.

Telephone directories frequently are used as sampling frames or lists because they are readily and cheaply available, frequently updated, accurate, and sometimes coincide with the geographic area of interest. They can, however, be inaccurate sampling frames in areas where residents are highly mobile and in urban areas with high rates of unlisted telephone numbers.

Random Lists of Telephone Numbers

Lists of telephone numbers, usually generated by a computer, are one of the more accurate sampling lists for interviewing the general population because they include unlisted numbers and new numbers. Obviously, they still miss the proportion of people who do not have telephones, which can be critical for surveys of some subpopulations. It usually is not that important, however, for most general-attitude public interest surveys.

The most frequent way of obtaining lists of telephone numbers is to use a computer program that generates random numbers for the appropriate area code and **central office code** (the second set of three digits after the area code in a ten-digit telephone number). Lists of randomly generated numbers, however, can be cumbersome to work with because of the high proportion of nonworking numbers. Purchasing these lists also can be expensive. Finally, lists of telephone numbers correspond well to some geographic areas and poorly to others. Area codes and telephone exchanges frequently cross congressional district boundaries, but exchanges rarely cross county lines, and area codes never cross state lines.

Because of the complexities of generating true random lists, we will not discuss here how to draw such a sample. However, you may want to consider buying such a sample from one of the many commercial firms that sell survey samples. Lists can be purchased or generated from working exchanges to cut down on the number of nonworking numbers.

WHOM WILL YOU MISS IN YOUR SAMPLE?

"No-phone" Households

When choosing telephone sampling, you should recognize that you are systematically going to miss some people. Roughly 5-7% of American households do not have telephones, and it is projected that this number will rise to 10-11% with the increase in telephone rates related to the breakup of AT&T (Dillman, 1978; Groves and Kahn, 1979; Kalton, 1983).

Households that lack telephones tend to be minority, southern, mobile households and those whose major breadwinner is under 35 years of age.

The nationwide average of unlisted telephone numbers is 20%, and this figure is increasing rapidly — up 25% in the last decade. The regional variation in unlisted numbers is enormous. For example, 40% of the numbers in New York City and 30% in California are unlisted. Your regional telephone office should be able to give you an estimate for your area. Individuals with unlisted telephone numbers tend to be younger, less educated, lower income, female, renters, and single or divorced.

Finally, error comes into some forms of telephone sampling because at any given time an average of 10% of working numbers are too new to be in directories. Obviously, this percentage is higher in more mobile areas. Also, 3% of households have multiple listings, which gives these households a disproportionate chance of getting into your sample. These households tend to be urban, eastern households and households with teenagers.

WHAT ABOUT "STRATIFYING" YOUR SAMPLE?

Overview

Sometimes certain population characteristics are important to the analysis of your study or to its strategic application. In this case, you should make sure that you get an adequate and accurate sample of those population subgroups as well as the population as a whole. This can be done by **stratifying** your sample: classifying your population into subgroups before the sample is drawn and then drawing minisamples proportionately from each strata or subgroup. The entire population must be classified into strata before you sample. The most common stratification method is by geographic characteristic (for example, stratifying a congressional district sample by precinct).

How to Stratify

To stratify a congressional district by precinct, you would pull a sample from each precinct after determining what proportion of the overall sample came from each precinct. Every precinct would be treated separately, and the sample would be drawn for each precinct without reference to other precincts but repeating the same sampling procedure for each precinct. Because sampling is essentially repetitive, this does not actually increase the work load as much as one might expect.

Stratification reduces the overall sampling error by ensuring that important population subgroups are represented proportionately in the sample. It also allows greater flexibility in sampling. For example, certain areas of particular interest could be oversampled.

WHAT SHOULD MY SAMPLE SIZE BE?

Sample Size

Sample size is usually dictated by:

- ☐ The precision required
- ☐ The number of interviewers and telephones available
- ☐ The cost of the survey
- ☐ The size and number of subgroups of interest
- ☐ The homogeneity of the population
- ☐ Your future goals for the sample. For example, if you are planning a panel poll, you will want to draw a larger initial sample because of attrition at each interview "wave."

 Important note: Contrary to popular belief, the error attached to a sample depends on the sample size, not on the size of the population from which the sample is drawn (for populations over 2500). Thus, a sample of 200 from a congressional district has the same error rate as a sample of 200 drawn from the United States. We recommend a sample size of no less than 200 completed interviews and samples of 400–500 for most major polls. As a consumer of polls, be sure to look at the sample size in evaluating the conclusions the authors have drawn. Is the sample size large enough to be representative? Are the differences they point out really within the margin of error? Making too much of a small difference is the most common trap analysts fall into.

Sample Error

A simple random sample of 200 has an error of ± 7%. A simple random sample of 500 has an error of ± 4.5%. For example, if you found in a poll of 200 registered voters that candidate *A* had 51% of the voters and candidate *B* had 49%, candidate *A's* actual vote in the population at the time of the poll could range from 44% to 58%. Table 7-1 shows the sampling error for a variety of sample sizes.

Remember we have been discussing only the **sampling error** — the error that comes from surveying a portion of the population rather than the entire population. It does not include any additional error that may come into the survey through bad question wording, poor interviewing, nonresponse problems (i.e., systematically missing certain kinds of people), or mistakes in data processing. We hope that other procedures, such as balanced questions, nondirective interviewing, call-backs, and refusal conversions, will keep this error random and minimal and thus will not systematically bias the results in one direction or another. Finally, by stratifying our sample, the actual error will be slightly less than these figures.

TABLE 7-1 *Sampling Error for Common Simple Random Samples**

Sample Size	Distribution of Opinion on Question		
	50%/50%	70%/30%	90%/100%
100	10%	9%	6%
200	7	6	4
300	6	5	3
400	5	4	3
500	4.5	4	2.5
700	4	3	2
1000	3	3	2

*Based on simple random samples with 95% confidence intervals.

Homogeneity of the Population

Table 7-1 has three columns of error calculations depending on the distribution of the responses to the question. Sampling error depends on the homogeneity of the population. If the population is homogeneous, sampling error is lower. Because most people in a homogeneous population are similar, we are unlikely to draw a sample that does not accurately reflect the population even if only a few people are interviewed. If opinions are widely divergent, there are more possibilities for error, and a bigger sample must be drawn to reflect accurately all that diversity.

Important note: In summarizing the error attached to the entire survey, use the column that refers to the maximum error (the error where opinions are split 50/50 and are thus most heterogeneous).

Confidence Intervals

Table 7-1 has calculated these sampling errors based on a **confidence interval** of 95%. This means that 95% of the time (or in 95 samples out of 100), the true or actual opinion in the population will be the sampled opinion plus or minus the error.

Some cheaper polls will quote you a lower sampling error than Table 7-1 for comparable sample sizes because they are using a lower confidence interval. Table 7-1 represents the standards for polls today and thus protects you as much as possible from erroneous conclusions.

Important note: Remember that the error is based on the size of the sample of completed interviews, not the size of the sample of telephone numbers or names you started out with before interviewing.

Subgroup Error

So far, this chapter has discussed the errors attached to the entire sample. If you are looking at the attitudes of a subsample of the population, the error for that subsample depends on its size. For example, if you have a sample of 200 teachers — 100 of whom are members of the American Federation of Teachers and 100 of whom are members of the National Education Association — and you are looking at the attitudes of NEA members toward merit pay, the error for that analysis is ± 10% (the error for a sample or subsample of 100), not ± 7% (the error for the entire sample of 200).

HOW DO YOU DISTRIBUTE YOUR SAMPLE?

Once you have determined your sample size, you may need to distribute that sample proportionately across subsamples if you are stratifying your sample. Following is a case study of how to do this for a legislative district sample stratified by precinct. In this case, the population is all registered voters in the district.

Case Study: Distributing A Sample

Take a district of 10,000 registered voters and three precincts: *A, B,* and *C.* Suppose precinct *A* has 5000 voters and therefore 50% of your district's registered voter population. You then would want 50% of your sample also to come from precinct *A* (i.e., 5000/10,000 = 50%). If precinct *B* has 3000 voters and therefore 30% of your district's total voters (3000/10,000 = 30%), 30% of your sample should come from precinct *B.* Finally, precinct *C* has 2000 voters, or 20% of the district's total voters (2000/10,000 = 20%), and therefore 20% of your sample should come from precinct *C.*

If you want a sample of 200 interviews, 100 of these interviews (i.e., 50% of the interviews, or 200 × 50% = 100) should come from precinct *A;* 60 interviews should come from precinct *B* (200 × 30% = 60); and 40 interviews (200 × 20% = 40) should come from precinct *C.* (Table 7-2 also presents these calculations.)

TABLE 7-2   *Calculating Sample Distribution*

	Precinct *A*	Precinct *B*	Precinct *C*	Total
Number of registered voters	5000	3000	2000	10,000
Percentage of total district's registration	50%	30%	20%	100%
Number of interviews for a total sample of 200	100	60	40	200

You have now determined the number of interviews you want and how they are distributed across precincts. If you draw your sample separately for each precinct (stratifying your sample by precinct), you are guaranteed of getting a valid sample at both the precinct and district levels.

Remember that when you look at the results for a single precinct in isolation, the sampling error for that precinct depends on the size of the sample in that precinct. For example, if you interviewed 100 voters from precinct *A,* you have an unbiased sample of precinct *A,* but it has an error rate of ±10% (the error attached to any sample of 100 people). The error rate for the analysis of your polling results within other subgroups in your poll would be calculated similarly.

HOW AND WHEN DO YOU DRAW AN OVERSAMPLE?

Overview

In most cases, you can reduce the sampling error in the analysis for a particularly important subgroup by interviewing a larger total sample, which will in itself increase the size of the subgroup proportionately, or oversampling respondents in that particular subgroup or strata if it is based on a classification you can use to stratify your sample.

As an example of oversampling: In a study of attitudes toward mining, you are particularly interested in the attitudes of respondents in the three counties hardest hit by a new coal company venture. Your overall sample of 500 respondents will only generate 75 interviews in these counties, with an error rate in that subgroup of ±11%.

You want to reduce that error rate to ±7%, or obtain 200 interviews in those three counties. Calculate the precision you want for that subgroup and thus the subgroup size you need (in this case, 200 interviews for an error rate of ±7%). In the oversampled subgroup you will sample with a higher fraction to obtain the extra interviews.

Case Study: Oversampling

Using the case described previously, first calculate how many interviews you will get in your regular sample (in the coal mining example it was 75) and how many cases are then in the oversample (in this case, 200 − 75, or 125). Now, increase your sampling fraction accordingly. For example, if the original sampling fraction for the entire study were 1 in 100, you would increase it to 1 in 37 for the three counties to obtain the oversample. After oversampling, randomly assign the interviews for the oversample subgroup into regular sample and oversample cases in the correct proportions — 75 cases in the sample and 125 cases in the oversample.

In your analysis of the total sample (in this case, statewide attitudes toward mining), you will want to exclude the oversample cases;

otherwise, you would throw off your conclusions about the total sample by overrepresenting a particular subgroup (the three counties). In your analysis of that subgroup, however, you would include these oversample cases and therefore reduce your sampling error for that analysis.

HOW DO YOU DRAW YOUR SAMPLE?

The easiest way to draw a sample is to use an existing list of eligible respondents, for example, a list of registered voters. To pick the names of the respondents who fall in your sample, you need to determine the **interval of selection,** or the **skip pattern,** randomly pick the first name to start from, and then choose each subsequent name that is the proper interval from the name previously selected. The interval of selection is chosen by dividing the total population size (i.e., the size of the list) by the sample size. In the previous example of 10,000 registered voters and a desired sample size of 200, the interval is calculated by dividing 10,000 by 200, which gives an interval of selection of 50. Thus, one voter out of 50 would be the designated respondent.

Note: Most of the time you will have to follow standard rounding rules in determining your interval. Such rounding may cause you to come out one or two names short at the end. In that case, treat your sample as if it were circular and go back around to the beginning of the sample to continue selecting the last names. You should not have to draw more than one or two names coming back through the list.

Random Start

To get the first name, pick a random number within the sampling interval, count down to that person from the beginning of the list, and use that name as your first respondent. In the example previously cited, pick a random number between 1 and 50 (for example, 9), and the ninth person on the list will be the first designated respondent. Then, every 50th person from that random starting point will be chosen — the 9th person on the list, the 59th person, the 109th person, and so on.

If your sample is stratified, pick a new random start for each strate, but keep the same interval. For our example, that would mean a new random start for each precinct. This ensures an independent, stratified sample.

 Important note: If you are oversampling in some strata or subgroup, you will change the interval accordingly for that strata, as well as the random start.

As with any sampling technique, once you have the sample selections, you need to transfer that information to coversheets for interviewers' use. If you are using a list such as registered voters without telephone numbers, you also will have to look those up and include them on the coversheets.

Fixed Interval Sampling

The kind of sampling described so far is called **fixed interval sampling,** or **systematic sampling,** which differs from **pure random sampling,** in which the names are mixed up and chosen randomly. Fixed interval sampling is easier to administer than pure random sampling. It works as well as long as there is no systematic ordering to your list (except for the order created by any stratification of your sample). If there is some other order in your list (for example, if all Hispanic persons are at the end of each precinct list), you may systematically miss some people by continually skipping over them with a fixed interval method.

 Important alert: Check your lists to make sure that such skipping is not a problem. If it is, you must mix the names on your list within strata.

 ### CHECKLIST—SAMPLING FROM LISTS

1. Decide on the relevant population for your survey topic.
2. Acquire a complete list of the population.
3. Decide on the sample size.
4. Use the sample and population sizes to calculate your sampling interval.
5. Stratify your sample if relevant.
6. Pick a random number within your sampling interval as your start.
7. Select your names, proceeding down the list.
8. Prepare your coversheets.

9. Calculate into the above procedures any adjustments for oversampling in any strata.

SAMPLING FROM DIRECTORIES

How to Sample from Directories

Sampling from directories is very similar to sampling from lists:

- ☐ Assemble a complete set of directories for your area.
- ☐ Estimate the size of your sample in each directory by counting the number of residential listings on an average page in the middle of the book and multiplying it by the number of pages per directory.
- ☐ Exclude large blocks of government listings from your count because you will be skipping nonresidential listings in your sample.
- ☐ Do not count multiple listings twice in your estimate.
- ☐ Calculate the proportion of numbers in your area in each directory if directories cut across the boundary of your interest area, and skip numbers outside your area of interest.

Once you have a count of the population represented by the directories and the proportion of that population in each directory, calculate your sampling interval, take a random start, and apply your interval as in sampling from any other list. If your sampling interval hits a nonresidential number, skip to the closest residential number, mark that as your sample unit, and continue your interval from there.

When calculating the size of the population in each directory, you may be unable to delete the nonresidential numbers and multiple listings. If that happens, when actually drawing the sample you should calculate your interval, take a random start, and apply your interval. However, if your sampling interval hits a nonresidential number, skip to the closest residential number, mark that as your sample unit, and go back to the initial nonresidential number you had originally landed on to continue counting your interval (otherwise, you may run out of names before your sample is fully drawn).

Important note: When you assemble all of the directories for a geographic area, some of the directories occasionally overlap in their listings of areas. This is particularly true in rural areas. These duplicate listings will have to be eliminated or skipped (i.e., treated as outside the area) in one of the directories. Otherwise, you will double the probability of selecting those households and thus bias your sample.

How to Do Add One Sampling

The add one design is a variation of directory designs that includes some aspects of random digit designs to improve coverage. It allows you to use directories as lists while sampling unlisted households. In the add one design, residential numbers are selected from a telephone directory and then one is added to the last digit of the sampled number to give us the actual sampled number to be called. This generates almost as high a percentage of working numbers as sampling directly from the telephone directory and avoids most non-residential numbers because such numbers are usually assigned in banks. It often does miss newer listings, however, which are also assigned in banks.

If your area is highly mobile or has a particularly high percentage of unlisted numbers, you will be forced to turn to buying or drawing a random digit sample because too many numbers will still be missed by this technique.

CHECKLIST—SAMPLING FROM DIRECTORIES

1. Decide on the relevant population for your topic.
2. Acquire all of the directories for that area.
3. Determine the number of names in each directory.
4. Decide on the sample size.
5. Use the estimates from the directories of the population size and the sample size to calculate your sampling interval.
6. Stratify your sample, if relevant.
7. Pick a random number within your sampling interval as your start.
8. Select your names, proceeding through the directories.
9. Prepare your coversheets.

HOW MANY NUMBERS DO YOU REALLY NEED TO SAMPLE TO GET YOUR SAMPLE SIZE?

Overview of Basic Calculations from a Projected Response Rate

Important note: Your sample size is your goal of completed interviews. Obviously, if you draw only as many names or sample units as your completed sample size goal, you will fall considerably short of your goal because of refusals, no answers, unlisted numbers, nonworking numbers, and so on.

The most common practice in polling is to estimate a response rate based on past experience of surveying, your type of sample, the quality of your list, and your knowledge of your local telephone system. Using all this information, you would calculate a **response rate** (i.e., the percentage of completed interviews you actually obtain from the number you try). Then you calculate how big a sample you need to draw to obtain your goal with that response rate.

Your estimate of your response rate includes assessments of loss from all sources: refusal, death, unlisted numbers, nonworking numbers, no answer after repeated call-backs, and so forth. Chapter 5 on Interviewing can give you some guidance on these estimates, but your own experience in your area is your best guide.

Most studies end up with response rates somewhere between 55% and 65% with the techniques we have discussed. Professional response rates range from 60% to 75%. Your response rate estimate should not be lower than 50%, even if this is your first in-house poll. Response rates under 50% often indicate a seriously biased sample because it means that the "average" person you contacted did not respond.

Important note: Some recent polling experience with samples drawn from registered voter lists produced a response rate of only 40-42%. We believe that the older the voter registration list, the higher the "respondent unavailability" due to moves, changed numbers, and the like. It would be wise to count on a slightly lower completion rate when dealing with voter registration lists that have not been updated or purged for several years.

Example: Let's assume for a sample drawn from a list of registered voters that you figured a 12% refusal rate (after refusal conversions are done), a 19% nonworking number and unlisted telephone rate, a 6% nonresponse rate due to not reaching anyone at the number despite repeated call-backs, and a 1% loss due to death and moving of respondents (i.e., respondent nonavailability). This adds up to a 37% nonresponse rate and an estimated 63% response rate. This means that for a sample of 200 completed interviews, you would need to draw 317 names (63% of the sample = 200 ÷ 0.63 = 317).

Note: You cannot stop calling numbers with this technique just because you have reached your targeted sample size. You must follow your call-back procedures for all the numbers to get an unbiased sample. You might end up with a slightly larger sample than you had planned. Obviously, considering time, costs, and error, it is important to be as accurate as possible in your estimates of response rates.

How to Do Replacement Sampling

Sampling based on response rates statistically introduces the least additional error into your sample. However, it is often difficult with volunteers and inexperienced pollsters to determine ahead of time what the response rate will be. This is why political polls in particular often do **replacement sampling.** In replacement sampling, initial respondents who do not generate a completed interview are replaced with other respondents who are expected to be very similar to the initial respondents on key attitudes for the study. For example, you would systematically replace respondents from lists of registered voters with other voters from their own precinct, called alternates.

Initially sampled voters are replaced by their first alternates *only* if they refuse, have unlisted or nonworking numbers, have died, or cannot be reached after four attempted calls. The second alternate is used *only* if the first alternate refuses, has an unlisted or nonworking number, or does not answer after three attempted call-backs at different times on different days.

Important note: You would never interview both alternates or the respondent and one of the alternates. Turning to replacements too early (i.e., before you have made repeated attempts to reach the initial respondent) will seriously bias the sample by including a disproportionate number of people who are easy to reach. These individuals tend to be more middle and upper income, female, older, and married or widowed. Interviewing more than one alternate or the respondent and an alternate is like interviewing a respondent twice and including both interviews in the sample.

Two to three alternates are designated for each sample respondent when the initial sample is chosen. With replacement sampling,
the number of initial sample respondents is the same as your goal
sample size for completed interviews. The replacement names are
given to the interviewer as well as the respondent's name. In fact, it
is good to put the whole unit on the coversheet (initial respondent
and two alternates).

When to Do Replacement Sampling

Replacement sampling is frequently abused and overused. It only
works when you are replacing respondents with similar people. In
most surveys, it is impossible to identify those people beforehand.
For some political surveys we feel fairly confident doing replacement
sampling because samples are picked from lists of registered voters
organized by precincts, and neighborhoods are usually politically
homogeneous. This means that replacing a respondent with someone systematically selected from within the same precinct is less likely to bias the samples.

Example—Choosing Replacements

Working with a list of registered voters, the most common procedure for choosing replacements is as follows:

To choose the first replacement, count down five names in the
voter registration list from the initial respondent. Pick the next
person of the same sex who is not at the same address as the initial
respondent. That may be the fifth name down from the designated
respondent, or you may have to skip down further to avoid members
of the same household. Don't worry about members of the same
family as long as they are registered at different addresses.

Highlight the name of the first replacement and put an "R1" next
to that name. The second replacement is chosen similarly and
marked with an "R2." Figure 7-1 is an example of a correctly
marked precinct list.

 Note: With this procedure, the replacements for a respondent always follow the respondent's name in the list. In all
cases, the replacements should be in the same precinct as
the respondent. If you come to the end of the list when choosing the

	63911	Aaberg, Albert 800 S. Black		80690	Bates, Mary 220 S. Jones
	63631	Aaberg, Mary 800 S. Black		84148	Beach, Harvey 22 S. Ewing
	86532	Abad, Lois 101 Cutler #14		63020	Beatty, Madie 110 S. Davis
	59738	Ackerman, Gaye J. 602 Brdwy		62686	Beatty, Marty 110 S. Davis
	59739	Ackerman, Paul 602 Brdwy		85545	Beaudry, Jon 441 S. Park
	78726	Ader, Barb 556 Spartan		76699	Beaurline, Addy 310 Blaker
	83013	Aiken, Ron 444 S. Davis		78320	Beaurline, Di 310 Blaker
	81617	Albin, Kerry 100 Blevins		77583	Beausolet, Ray 3 S. Rhode
	40958	Allinson, Barb 530 N. Fee		84934	Beaver, Joe 5993 Parker
*	77100	Allinson, Bob 530 N. Fee		76008	Beckstron, Ron 517 Cooke
	84839	Allinson, Dave 530 N. Fee		13308	Belgard, Vi 204 Mount
	84932	Allinson, Ted 530 N. Fee		78916	Bell, Delle 560 W. Main
	75152	Ames, David 18 Chaucer		73640	Bell, Steve 560 W. Main
R1	49958	Anderberg, Anne 115 Chaucer		55571	Bennett, Shirley 30 Black
	26907	Anders, Henry 600 3rd		42431	Bennett, Tim 30 Black
	26705	Anders, Jean 600 3rd		82103	Benson, Brad 540 Hill
	85896	Anders, Kimberly 600 3rd		77218	Benson, Jill 540 Hill
	81468	Anderson, Carol 310 Tree		76429	Bentley, Jim 17 S. Davis
	86326	Anderson, Karl 100 State	*	49204	Berg, Clayton 773 N. Hill
	51274	Anderson, Larry 516 Davis		62418	Bernard, Irene 411 State
R2	75780	Anderson, Lisa 30 Division		62678	Bernard, Alan 411 State
	86933	Andes, Rob 212 N. Park		74061	Betts, Rob T. 415 S. Fee
	86448	Andrew, Janes 210 Pine		73859	Betts, Susan 415 S. Fee
	64907	Andrew, Jack 210 Pine	R1	81909	Beyrau, Jon 4773 Hillard
	24940	Annat, Sara 100 S. State		84717	Bilar, Abe 2022 Mount
	79520	Applegreen, Bob 107 Park		84716	Bilar, Sumya 2022 Mount
	86378	Armstrong, Catie 510 Brdwy		6652	Binker, Anna 515 11th
	74786	Artzen, Melanie 570 Jerome		84149	Bishop, Tanya 322 Davis
	86742	Asken, Sidney 24 S. Broad		70078	Bjornsen, Bjorg 3 Tremont
	76936	Atkinson, Aubrey 415 Fee		84935	Blackman, Beth 811 Brdwy
				56108	Blankenship, Barb 14 Fee
	76875	Babbitt, Greg 107 Brdwy	R2	56109	Blankenship, Thom 14 Fee
	78637	Ballard, Robert 10 Miller		6078	Blewett, J. P. 6334 Mount
	81159	Baraby, Bobbi 555 10th		86075	Block, Jeff 733 N. Hillard
	25856	Barnes, Lilly 600 Broad		81160	Bloom, Dave 1120 N. 11th
	20561	Barnes, Brent 600 Broad		81161	Bloom, Sue 1120 N. 11th
	83374	Barningham, Jes 3 N. 3rd		83375	Bobothe, Dan 22 N. Karl
	21866	Basinger, Mrs. G. 4 N. 1st		80388	Bock, Phyllis 117 Blaker
	21865	Basinger, George 4 N. 1st		84936	Boret, Kim 566 E. 5th St
	81941	Basinger, Tom 4 N. 1st		84892	Boret, Patrick 566 E. 5th
	80689	Bates, Daryn Overseas		70538	Bolecham, Billy 750 Pine

Note: Anderson, Karl was not chosen as the second replacement name for Allinson, Barb, even though it was the fifth name following the first replacement name. It was not chosen because the respondent was not the same gender as the designated respondent (female). Count down until you come to the first respondent of the same gender after at least five names.

FIGURE 7-1 *Sample of first page of list of registered voters in precinct A.*
The * in this list indicates the designated respondent; R1 is the first replacement; and R2 is the second replacement. In this table, nine is the random starting point, and *every fiftieth name is chosen as a respondent.*

replacements for the last designated name, simply wrap around and continue counting from the beginning of the precinct list. You should only need to do this for the last name.

Replacement sampling also is possible but much less desirable with directories unless you use crisscross directories that list people by address. Without crisscross directories, you have little chance of replacing the initial respondent with a similar individual.

HOW TO SELECT THE RESPONDENT WITHIN THE HOUSEHOLD

Important note: Except when sampling from lists of individuals, getting the household telephone number is only half the battle; we also have to decide whom to interview within the household.

A variety of techniques can be used to randomly select the individual within the household. Random selection is necessary because most surveys try to generalize about the range of attitudes of the full population of individuals, assuming that people within households may have different opinions.

Overview

All techniques for sampling within the household require getting some information from the person who answers the telephone about the adult members of the household. Selection tables randomly assigned to each coversheet or general rules implemented by the interviewers then tell the interviewer who should be questioned.

The choice of the respondent is never left up to the discretion of the interviewer. To maintain the representative probability sample, all adults in the household must have a known probability of being selected into the sample. This would be impossible if interviewers were allowed to choose the respondent by whim or availability. Technically, respondents within a household have a known but not equal chance of being selected into a sample with the household selection methods we will discuss. The more adults there are in the household, the less likely they are to be selected as a respondent. Some studies weight for this unequal probability of selection, but it rarely makes a difference and thus can be ignored in your studies.

Problems

With most representative sampling techniques, the person who answers the telephone is often not the one who ends up being the respondent. It takes thorough training and skill for interviewers to implement these household sampling techniques and elicit the household information without getting a refusal.

Interviewers often believe that they are severely disadvantaged in obtaining the interview if they do not know beforehand the name of the respondent (as in a sample from a list of registered voters) or at least the name of the household (as in a sample from directories). Refusal rates, however, are not higher if interviewers are confident and well trained. Sending letters introducing the study to respondents before the interviewer calls (a practice more common in personal surveys) does lower initial refusal rates by as much as 50% (Dillman, 1978). Unfortunately, public interest groups rarely have the resources and time to do this before conducting a study.

QUOTA SAMPLING

Quota sampling is a common method of choosing respondents within households and is frequently used by commercial firms in quick and dirty polls. It is cheap, easy, fast, and avoids obvious bias in the sample. Unfortunately, it can introduce serious bias which only becomes obvious when you start an in-depth analysis of your results.

Sex Quota

In the most common form of quota sampling, interviewers are instructed to make sure that half of the people they interview are women and half are men. They can interview whoever answers the telephone as long as that person is 18 years of age or older. If interviewers start to get more female respondents than males, they are told to ask to speak to someone in the household who is male and over 18 (vice versa, of course, if they are getting more male respondents).

Within those constraints, interviewers can poll anyone who is willing and available. Some polls add the additional constraint that interviewers must actually alternate the sex of the respondent on each call unless the household called had only one eligible adult in it.

Age Quota

In political surveys of registered voters, an additional quota is often added for age because it is so difficult to get surveys of registered voters that do not underrepresent young voters. (Obviously, these filters all refer to samples not already drawn from lists of individual registered voters.)

After the introduction, interviewers ask, "Is there anyone in your home between 18 and 24 years of age who is registered to vote at this address?" If the answer is "yes," the interviewers ask, "May I please speak with him or her?"

If the young person is not available, refuses the interview, or there is no one in the household 18-24 years old who is registered to vote, the interview proceeds with the person who answered the telephone or the person chosen by the other quota questions.

Problems

Quota sampling tries to avoid blatant bias by preventing surveys with 75% female respondents, for example. However, it is incorrect to assume that this method truly generates a representative sample. Quota sampling disproportionately interviews those who are easy to reach, want to be interviewed, and answer the telephone. These samples thus tend to oversample older people, especially older women, people not employed outside the home, and people who are not the heads of households. Depending on the topic of your survey, this can indeed be a serious bias.

Quota samples are a specific example of a whole type of sample called nonprobability designs. In **nonprobability designs** (as opposed to probability designs, discussed in this chapter), every person in the population does not have a known and equal chance of being included in the sample. For example, a woman over 24 who never answers the telephone has virtually no chance of being selected into the sample for her household in the example we have been discussing. It's a shame to go to all of the work of drawing a solid probability sample and then inject bias at the point of sampling within households (an unknown and unmeasured amount of bias at that).

It is a particular shame because there are relatively easy methods of probability respondent selection. If implemented correctly, these probability designs do not bias your sample.

Birthday Quotas: Some groups are still drawn to quota sampling for respondent selection within households because it is easy to administer with volunteers. If you decide to use a quota sample, the best by far is what is popularly called the birthday method. With this method, after the introduction the interviewer asks to speak to the person over age 18 living in this household who has had the most recent birthday. If that person is not available, the interviewer finds out his or her name and when to call back to speak with that person.

Although still a nonprobability design, the birthday method is a vast improvement over other quota designs because it is not dependent on who answers the telephone. It is more difficult than some quota designs because it often requires setting up appointments with respondents who are not at home at the time of the initial contact. But it is much more representative of the total population for that reason.

PROBABILITY HOUSEHOLD LISTING—MODIFIED TRODAHL/CARTER DESIGNS

Overview

Most probability designs or within-household selection require getting a complete listing of who is in the household before the respondent can be selected. This can prove time-consuming and cumbersome and requires extensive training of the interviewers. Interviewers also believe it increases the refusal rate, although this has not been found to be true in actual experiments with well-trained interviewers.

Trodahl and Carter and others have developed a probability method that is statistically sound and does not require a full listing of the household.

How to Do a Modified Trodahl/Carter Design

The modified Trodahl/Carter design uses six selection tables to choose the respondent. These selection tables should be randomly assigned to and printed on the coversheets of the sample such that one sixth of the sample has version 1 of the table, one sixth has version 2, and so on. The six tables appear in Appendix A of this book. The selection tables determine the sex and relative age of the respondent to be interviewed.

The probabilities underlying the Trodahl/Carter selection tables are based on census estimates of the general population. If your population does not resemble the national census population, your sample may be seriously biased by using this method. In that case you should definitely use the Kish full-household listing method (Kish, 1965), which is not discussed in this book.

In the modified Trodahl/Carter design, after the introduction, the interviewer proceeds with a series of questions used to select the respondent. The questions should be printed on the coversheet along with the selection table. The interviewer marks the responses to the questions on the coversheet and chooses the respondent accordingly. The following example shows how questions are used to select the respondent:

Example—Selecting Respondents With Modified Trodahl/Carter

Version 1 of the selection tables in Appendix A has been marked for this example. The instructions to the interviewers are capitalized:

1. Now, could you tell me how many people total, including yourself, live in this household? (MARK ANSWER ON LINE: _____.)
2. How many of the people living here, including yourself, are 18 years of age or older? (CIRCLE NUMBER ON TOP OF SELECTION TABLE.)
3. How many of these are women? (CIRCLE NUMBER IN LEFT MARGIN OF SELECTION TABLE.)

For this survey, I would like to speak to the (VERBAL LABEL INDICATED ON GRID IN THE SELECTION TABLE) currently living at home in your household. Is he (or she) at home? (Appendix A contains the selection tables that would usually appear on the coversheet after these questions, with one selection table randomly assigned to each coversheet.)

Suppose you are calling a household in which a married couple, their 10-year-old child, and the wife's mother live. The wife answers the call. She should respond that there are four people in the household, three adults (which you would mark as in version 1 of the selection table in Appendix A), and two women. Looking at the intersection of the number of adults in the household and the number of women on the selection table, you would in this case ask to speak to the youngest woman over 18 (i.e., the wife).

Some surveys exclude the first question in the interviewer series we have given because it is really only used as a frame of reference for the respondent. However, including this question significantly improves the accuracy of this method by helping to eliminate the tendency of respondents to underestimate the size of large households and to miss children age 18–21 (Groves and Kahn, 1979).

FILTERS

Overview

Sometimes the sampling is not finished with the selection of the respondent within the household. Frequently, we want to limit the population to a certain subgroup, but we cannot identify that subgroup before we actually talk to possible respondents. Thus, the first few questions are used to screen desired respondents from the population. The most common cases are polls of registered voters or likely voters that are samplings from the general population using **RDD** (random digit dialing) methods or directory designs. Filters are then used to limit respondents to members of the subgroup of interest.

Registered Voters Filter

If you want to interview only registered voters, your interviewer asks the respondent already selected by one of the previous methods, "Are you registered to vote at this address?" If the answer is "yes," the interviewer proceeds. If the answer is "no" or "not sure," the interview is terminated.

If you are using the birthday quota, or modified Trodahl/Carter, do not look for another registered voter in the household. If you are using a simple sex quota method, you may choose to have the interviewers ask, "Is there a registered voter at home with whom I might speak?"

You can filter your sample using any criteria — demographic characteristics, geographic location, report of past behavior, and so on, or you can use a set of questions to identify certain people.

Calculating Sample Size and Response Rate with Filtered Samples

If you use a filter to finish defining the population for your sample, do not count interviews you terminate against your response rate. These interviews do not belong to the sample and are not counted as refusals or nonresponses. Also, if you are using a sampling technique based on an estimate of your response rate (see discussion earlier in this chapter), try to estimate how many interviews you will terminate as nonsample and increase the number of names or telephone numbers sampled accordingly.

For example, suppose you want a sample of 200 registered voters. You have estimated that your response rate will be 65%. Of that, you will actually interview only 80% of the respondents you call because 20% will not prove to be registered voters (using your filters). That means that you would need to initially draw 385 names $[(200 \div 0.65) \div 0.8 = 385]$.

HOW DO YOU EVALUATE YOUR SAMPLE?

There are two issues in evaluating your sample. The first is to evaluate beforehand the kind of sample you want to draw in order to choose the appropriate method of sampling. Then you need clearly and specifically to define the population you want to sample for your study so you can evaluate the noncoverage problems and bias with each method.

Choosing the Sampling Technique

All sampling should be evaluated in terms of your group's resources, including access to telephones and lists, the interviewers you have (their experience and number), the time you have, the kind of expert advice available to you, the kind of population that interests you and its fit with existing lists, the telephone system in your area (including the proportion of nonworking, new, and unlisted numbers), and the level of accuracy you need given how you are going to use your polling information.

The most important thing to do is to come to a good understanding of your choices in sampling techniques, what they involve in implementation, and what tradeoffs you are making with the selection of each method.

Evaluating Bias and Representativeness

After completing your poll, you also will want to evaluate how representative your sample is. To do that, you want to run frequencies on your basic demographic questions such as age, sex, education, and race to see how closely your poll reflects the population sampled. If your study is of the general population, you can compare these distributions to census data to see how you did. You also can compare your frequencies to those in other polls.

Sloppy or incorrect sampling procedures are the first thing you should look for in evaluating someone else's polls. Did everyone in the population have a chance of being interviewed or just people who were easily accessible? Some common problems are:

☐ Missing people who have unlisted numbers in areas with highly mobile people or high rates of unlisted telephones.
☐ Interviewing the first person who answers the telephone rather than choosing within the household.
☐ Systematically missing people who are home only on weekends.

Careful sampling and interviewing techniques can minimize these biases. As a consumer of polls, you can judge the survey both by the description of the sample and the demographic profile of the respondents. Always check to see if some group seems over- or underrepresented. Common problems are too many women, too few young people, and too many older people — reflecting who is easiest to reach.

Weighting Your Sample

Commercial polls frequently weight their data to force their polls to reflect the known demographic profile of the population if their polls are off. Weights are discussed briefly in Chapter 8 on Processing Data, although POLLSTART, the software package designed to complement this book, does not allow for weighting data.

Although weighting may make you more comfortable with the survey and facilitate analysis, it does not overcome the bias introduced into a survey by systematically missing certain kinds of people. That bias can only be avoided early in the survey process by good sampling and interviewing techniques. As a consumer of polls, you should be suspicious of a survey that seems heavily weighted. Look for a description of what weighting has been done.

✓ CHECKLIST—DRAWING A SAMPLE

1. What is the population you are interviewing?
2. What list are you using for your sampling frame?
3. Are you stratifying your sample?
4. What is your sample size?
5. Are you drawing an oversample?
6. What is the sampling error attached to your total sample and to your most important analytical subgroups?
7. What method are you using to draw your sample: lists, directories, randomly generated telephone numbers, and so on?
8. Are you using replacement sampling?
9. If you are not using replacement sampling, have you calculated a probable response rate and thus how many households you need to sample?
10. How are you selecting the actual respondent within the sample household?
11. Do you need a filter for your questionnaire to implement the full sample design?
12. Have you prepared your coversheets with the sampling information, replacement sample (if required), and household selection table (if required)?

CHAPTER EIGHT

Processing Data: Methods and Options

GETTING THE DATA READY FOR TABULATION

Editing

The first step in getting the data ready for tabulation is editing the questionnaires. Editing involves checking through each question of each completed questionnaire to make sure all answers are ready to be coded and entered (either into the computer or onto hand-tabulation grids).

Every question (if you are using our software) or every column (for other software) should have one and only one numeric code attached to it. The numeric code corresponds to the answer given by the respondent for the question. When checking through the questionnaires, you may find that some answers are missing. You will need to fill in the appropriate missing data codes for questions that have been skipped. The missing data code is usually "9" for "not ascertained" ("NA") or inappropriate "INAP" for correctly skipped questions.

 Remember: When you are editing, be sure to assign and enter into the data file a unique identification number to each questionnaire so you can retrieve individual cases as well as responses to questions across cases.

Coding

For most close-ended questions, the **coding** (transfer of a verbal response to a numeric code) will be obvious because it is the number given by the respondent or the number attached to the answer chosen.

For open-ended questions, where the interviewers actually wrote down the response and did not precode it, you will need to develop a coding scheme. This is done by looking at the clustering of the responses offered or by turning to a standard code; for example, a standard occupational groupings code developed by the U.S. Department of Labor. Some presurvey planning can help in the development of these codes as you try to identify the categories you would expect people to use when they answer.

The most common mistake in developing open-ended codes is using too many categories. The analysis becomes meaningless because each category receives too few cases. A rule of thumb is that each category should have at least 10% of the cases unless it is particularly important to note that very few people responded in a certain way.

You may decide to add a category to a code once you start coding. This should be done carefully. If you decide to do this, you must return to previously coded questionnaires to code the new category where it now applies.

 One final note: Whoever does the coding should be trained, checked, and supervised to keep the influence of coding as unbiased as possible. As with interviewing, the coding of a question should be the same regardless of who codes it.

Data Files

After coding and editing are done, take a copy of the questionnaire and note on it the added codes (missing data, for example) and the codes for the open-ended questions. This will become your master answer sheets, or **codebook.**

Next, decide the missing values for each question — the values you want to exclude from all or most of your percentage calculations. As a basic rule, these usually include the codes for answers that were skipped:

☐ "NA" codes — response codes for questions that were
   unintentionally skipped ("not ascertained")
☐ "INAP" codes — response codes that were intentionally
   skipped ("inappropriate")
☐ "Don't know" responses

In other words, your analysis usually focuses on people who have opinions. Be sure to make a note of the missing data and missing value codes in your codebook.

Important note: You will need to consult the guide to your software for such factors as width restrictions in entering data, missing data codes, variable numbers and names for questions, and so on. Every data software package will provide details on its data entry restrictions. For example, POLLSTART, the software designed to complement this book, limits the width of variables to two columns and numeric characters, excluding the zero. Many software packages also will produce a codebook (POLLSTART does through its "LIST" function).

Cleaning Data

Cleaning the data ensures that all data are correct and consistent. Basically, whether using hand or computer tabulation, **consistency checking** involves checking for invalid or wild codes, codes that were not used for any answer in a question, or answers that are inconsistent with other answers. For example, someone who responded they had no children should not later be coded as responding that the age of their oldest child was 24 years. When inconsistencies are identified, you should examine the questionnaire to determine the correct codes, and then correct the data.

If you are doing computer tabulation, your software package will allow you to go back and change values for specific questions for specific respondents (using their identification number and the question or variable number). Many software packages, including POLLSTART, will alert you to invalid or wild codes as they are entered into the computer data file.

It often is possible to clean much of the data in the process of editing because inconsistencies and wild codes are apparent if you check questionnaires carefully.

HAND TABULATION

Hand tabulation is feasible only if you have a very short questionnaire and basic information needs. This method is most helpful if you anticipate your analysis needs as much as possible and tabulate the needed information in one pass through your questionnaires. A sample hand-tabulation grid is included and discussed in Appendix C. The easiest way to hand tabulate questionnaires is to set up a grid to categorize each respondent's answers. Then photocopy these grids for use by all of your coders. After all the questionnaires have been tabulated, the responses are added and percentages calculated.

COMPUTER TABULATION

In most cases, after your data have been edited, you will need to set up a computer data file according to your software package. Enter the data from the completed questionnaires and clean the data of any inconsistencies or wild or invalid codes. If your questionnaire is carefully planned, you can enter data directly from the completed questionnaires themselves.

If there is a "verification" function in your software, you also should verify your data before beginning any tabulation. A verification function has you enter the data twice. The program then checks the two entries to see if they are the same. The POLLSTART verification requires that the data be entered a second time. The program will automatically alert you to discrepancies in the two sets of data.

For anything but the simplest questionnaire, computer tabulation is faster, more flexible, more accurate, and capable of richer analyses. After your data file is set up, proceeding with initial computer analysis is much like setting up a hand-tabulation grid.

You will want at least two types of analyses:

□ **Frequency distributions** (lists of the number of respondents who gave *each* answer to each question) for every answer to every question (sometimes called raw data or counts). For example, Men respondents: 257; Women: 271.

□ **Cross tabulations** (bivariate frequency distributions that show simultaneously the relationship between the responses to two questions) of responses with categories or subgroups identified in other questions. For example, number of women who support the sales tax: 79 and 29%.

This is commonly called setting up your basic **break** or **banner run.** For example, in a political survey, you will want to see two-way tables or cross tabulations of most questions by your basic political and social subgroups, including gender, age, union membership,

region, race, educational level, party identification, political interest, and vote intention. For example, here is a cross tabulation from
POLLSTART:

For the question on how respondents by gender feel about the sales
tax, the cross tabulation would be:

    sales tax question by gender (M/F).
    (support, non-support, don't know . . . by . . . male or female)

	TOTAL	Men	Women
TOTAL	100%/528	100%/257	100%/271
1.1 Support	46%/241	63%/162	29%/79
1.2 Non-Support	44%/233	32%/82	56%/151
1.3 Don't Know	10%/54	5%/13	15%/41

In these runs, the computer will sort respondents into groups, add
up groups, take percentages, and print out results. Samples of cross
tabulations produced by the POLLSTART program are included in
Appendix D.

The POLLSTART software designed to complement this book is
interactive. Rather than entering an entire set of requests for cross
tabulations (commands) at once, you can enter them one at a time
as you proceed with your analysis. You also can set up a series of
runs at once that the computer will execute automatically using a
"Submit" or "DO" command. (These programs are part of the
CP/M and DOS operating systems and also may be included in your
own computer software package.)

CREATING NEW MEASURES FROM SEVERAL QUESTIONS

In telephone surveys, in particular, it is common to break one question into several parts that are easier for respondents to answer.
Later, these parts should be combined into one series of coded
answers for analysis. Most software packages allow some recoding
of answers for this purpose. Combining and recoding of questions
requires thought and planning but results in richer and more complete analyses.

The most common example of what is needed is the question on party identification. First, respondents are asked if they consider themselves Republicans, Democrats, or what. Then, Republicans are asked if they consider themselves weak or strong Republicans (and Democrats likewise). Independents then are asked if they lean toward the Democratic or Republican party. In analyzing the issues, however, these two questions are recoded into one question with answer codes like:

1. Strong Republican
2. Weak Republican (includes Independent leaning to Republican)
3. Pure Independent (answer "Independent" to both)
4. Weak Democrat (includes Independent leaning to Democrat)
5. Strong Democrat

The answers for questions about age, income, number of children, age of children, and feelings toward political figures often are obtained as exact numbers. These exact numbers are of little use in analysis and need to be combined into broader categories during the precoding or coding stages. For example:

Age codes:
1. 18–25
2. 25–35
3. 35–45
4. 45–55
5. 55–65
6. Over 65

Also, some questions will be asked in a series. For example, you might ask what different types of media are used as information sources. You will want to look both at the separate answers and at the combined question that would give you, for example, a total number of media sources used (respondent uses zero, one, two, three, or four total media sources).

Recoding needs to be planned carefully but should come naturally if you have prepared your study objectives well.

 Important note: Planning is particularly necessary with the POLLSTART software designed to complement this book because it does not allow questions to be recoded or added once data have been entered. Some other software packages will allow you to do this after the data entry stage.

✓ CHECKLIST—PROCESSING DATA

1. Do you have any open-ended questions? Have you developed codes for them from standard codes or from the completed questionnaires?
2. Have you edited the questionnaires? Do you have a numeric code for every question and only one numeric code per question?
3. Did you decide what the "missing data" values for each question are?
4. Have you checked your data once they have been run for invalid codes and inconsistencies?
5. Have you set up your hand tabulation grids or thought out your basic data breaks or cross tabulations?
6. What questions do you want to combine to form a new set of categories? Have you anticipated at what stage and how you are going to do this recoding?

CHAPTER NINE

Analysis

WHAT DO YOU WANT TO KNOW?

Before you begin your poll, you have in mind certain things you want to know. For example, you might want to find out what the public thinks about the Coalition to Protect the Environment (COPE). The questionnaire must be designed carefully so you find out what you really want to know without biasing the results. You want the truth as best it can be discerned, not an agreeable fiction that may lead you to make wrong decisions on the basis of the poll.

Most important, ask yourself why you want the information. Perhaps you are going to do a public education campaign or a membership drive. In that case, you want to know not only what the public thinks of COPE, but some of the factors influencing their perceptions.

Are certain parts of the population down on your group? Why? That information would be important in an education campaign. Are other segments favorably disposed toward you? That knowledge would be important in a membership campaign.

In short, know beforehand what you really want to know, and ascertain whether the poll is going to tell you what you really need to know. You should look at other groups' polls from the same perspective. Did they ask the follow-up questions really necessary to justify their conclusions? Earlier chapters in this book will help you to evaluate the methodology of polls conducted by other groups. The problems in polls, however, often come at the analysis and interpretation stage. This chapter should help give you a critical and systematic eye for examining the conclusions made by other groups.

RULES OF REPORTING — WRITING UP THE ANALYSIS

There are certain basic things you should include in your analysis report and look for in critiquing others' reports of their polling data. Somewhere in the report there should be a short description of:

- ☐ The type of sample
- ☐ The sample size
- ☐ The type of interview
- ☐ The interviewing period

Your conclusions should be written up, along with the presentation of the appropriate data from which these conclusions are drawn. This allows readers to judge whether you have interpreted the findings correctly. All tables should include percentages and some indication of the number of cases used in the analysis. Included somewhere in the analysis, at least in the appendix, should be the exact wording of the key questions. Most important, you need to show by the patterns of the answers why you have drawn certain conclusions. This is easier said than done, of course. The inexperienced analyst can easily make mistakes such as placing too much emphasis on small differences, drawing too broad a conclusion from the data presented, or ignoring an intervening relationship.

THE BASIC ANALYSIS

Answers and Percentages

The first step in data analysis is to run **frequency distributions,** the answers and percentages for the questions. For example:

```
1. How do you feel about the Coalition to Protect the Environment?
   (n = 207)
   A. Positive            53%/106
   B. Neutral             10%/20
   C. Negative            17%/34
   D. Don't know          20%/40
   E. Missing data           7
```

This sort of result is given for every question. It gives the percentage for each answer, as well as the number of actual answers. Even more important, "n = 207" tells you the total number of respondents. After subtracting the missing data (7), you have 200 respondents answering a question, with nearly 50% being favorable toward COPE, and 50% feeling otherwise. As discussed in Chapter 7 on Sampling, the answer is ± 7% (the sampling error) at a 95% confidence level. This means we are 95% sure that the percentage of the public who feel positive toward COPE right now is between 46% (53% − 7%) and 60% (53% + 7%). An alternative way of saying this is that if everyone were interviewed, 95 times out of 100 the population's positive feeling toward COPE will fall between 46% and 60%.

One could also conclude from the answers that a substantial number (53%) of people like COPE, although there is no way of knowing from this question how positive they are or why. The organization has been doing something controversial enough for 17% of the public to feel negatively toward it, and only 20% of the public doesn't know the group, which shows that the group has been in the public eye.

Cross tabulations

In the next phase of data analysis, cross tabulations or two-way tables of the opinion and behavior questions are run against demographic questions to see how answers differ by important subgroups. For example, a "cross tab" might look like this:

	TOTAL	WOMEN	MEN
TOTAL		100%/110	100%/90
Feelings toward COPE			
Positive	53%	43%/47	66%/59
Neutral	10%	14%/15	6%/5
Negative	17%	14%/15	21%/19
Don't know	20%	30%/33	8%/7
(Key: 43%/47 = %/number of actual respondents)			

The first row of numbers reveals that of the 200 respondents for which we have data, 110 are women and 90 are men. The next row shows that 53% of the whole sample are positive toward COPE. Of these individuals, 43% (or 47) of the women, and 66% (or 59) of the men, are positive in their feelings toward COPE. Thus, men are more positive than women.

In your analysis, you should distinguish what is significant and what is not. For instance, a higher percentage of men (21%) than of women (14%) feel negative about the group. However, there is a possible sampling error of ±7% for the whole sample. Because the number of men and women involved is 90 and 110, respectively, the sampling error within those groups is closer to ±10% for questions with answers in the range of 50/50. These negative answers are in the range of 80/20 (20% negative, 80% all others), so the sampling error is ±8%.

This means that the negative rating by the women might be as high as 22% and as low as 13% by men. In other words, the correct conclusion about negative ratings toward COPE is that it is impossible to tell any significant difference between the attitudes of men and women by this poll, although men *might* be somewhat more negative.

An easy way to begin picking out what is statistically important is to calculate the sampling error for the whole sample using the information given in Chapter 7 on Sampling. For 200 respondents, the sampling error would be ±7%. Then circle every subgroup answer that varies from the total sample value by more than that. If 53% of the public were positive toward COPE circle every answer lower than 46% or higher than 60%. This rule of thumb reveals that the difference as to who is positive toward the group is significant. Men appear to be more favorably inclined toward COPE than women. This is statistically significant, and should be a useful finding if this poll is intended to raise consciousness or increase membership.

On the neutral answers, we are looking for percentages higher than 17% or lower than 3%. This is not the case; therefore, the apparently higher neutrality of women is meaningless because it could easily be the "luck of the draw" in the people who were chosen for the sample.

On the negative answers, we are looking for answers higher than 24% or lower than 10%. Again, the apparent negativity of the men is statistically insignificant — no conclusion can be drawn from it.

The "Don't know" answers are more than 7% away from the average answer, however. It is statistically significant that more women don't know COPE than men.

This cross tabulation yields two solid findings:

1. That men are more positive toward COPE.
2. That women are less likely to know anything about the group.

COMMON MISTAKES IN ANALYSIS

When analyzing your own results or those of another organization, there are certain common mistakes you should be aware of.

Overanalyzing Results

Important note: Although polling is a powerful tool, there's a limit to what it can tell you. Most relationships in a poll are fairly weak and should be interpreted as such.

Overanalysis means drawing conclusions that are not warranted by the data. The most common ways of doing this are ignoring sampling error, giving undue importance to meaningless relationships, and overstating cause and effect.

Ignoring Sampling Error

The common temptation is to assume that if a higher percentage of men are negative toward COPE, that men are more negative than women toward the group. But we have shown that the difference is within the range of sampling error (at a 95% confidence). That is, if 100 identical polls were taken at the same time, 95 of them would have answers for each question within the range of error indicated. Five out of 100 would have answers even farther from the truth than the sampling error quoted.

If 200 people are polled and 53% of them say they feel positive toward COPE, you can be relatively certain the actual percentage of the public at large is between 46% and 60%. The difference is due solely to luck, assuming that the sample is drawn correctly and that nothing else in the polling process biases the answers. Therefore, polls give us only good guesses about what everyone is thinking at a particular point in time.

As mentioned previously, for a sample of 200, the sampling error is ± 7%. This is a rough guide you can use when checking significant answers. However, any time the sample is broken down, such as into men and women, we actually have a higher sample error. For a category or subsample size of 100, the sampling error is ± 10%. The sampling error also varies depending on whether the distribution of opinion among the answers is about 50/50 (50% one answer and 50% another) or closer to 90/10.

There are two ways to keep on track without having to be concerned about the actual statistical parameters of each answer. The first is to circle all the answers that are outside the statistical variation for the whole sample (± 7% for a sample of 200). The second is to ignore all subsamples that involve fewer than 50 people because the error would be too great (not all *answers,* but all subsamples or subgroups). For example, in the COPE sample, there were 90 men and 110 women. If you had taken a cross tabulation involving professions, you might have come out with these numbers of respondents: 75 blue-collar workers, 53 managers, 12 self-employed people, 18 unemployed individuals, 24 who work at home, and 18 teachers. No matter how the unemployed, the teachers, and those who work at home answered, you should ignore their answers. You simply do not have enough responses to draw any valid conclusions.

You can avoid this by setting up your answers so you don't have categories that are too small. The most common mistake in this direction is to ask for a person's occupation and then have ten or more different categories. Make your answer categories broad enough so that the responses in each category will be statistically meaningful.

Giving Undue Importance to Meaningless Relationships

You may discover that there are very similar percentages of people who like COPE and people who eat pickles for breakfast (if you have a large and rambling poll). Common sense tells you there is no meaningful relationship between the two concepts, so it doesn't make sense to waste time trying to see if the correspondence between COPE and pickles holds true for different segments of the public.

Overstating Cause and Effect

Polls give us certain numbers with a fixed degree of certainty, but it is important not to conclude too much about the cause and effect of those numbers. We can say a lot about what things are associated or related, but we can only speculate and rarely prove much about what causes a given attitude or behavior with polling data.

People analyzing polling data also often make unwarranted conclusions about intensity of feeling when they only have evidence of a position's popularity. For example, if 53% of the people feel positive toward COPE, that does not say anything about how strongly they feel on the issue. We can certainly not conclude that a good membership drive will wind up with 53% of the population paying dues to the association.

Multiple Mentions

Another common mistake is made when questions with multiple mentions (more than two answers) are added up. For example, suppose you have a poll of two respondents who were asked to list the three most important problems facing the state today. Half the respondents give three economic issues and half the respondents give education, the environment, and women's rights. If we incorrectly added the results, we might conclude that education was not a very important problem because it was only one of six answers. However, half of the respondents mentioned education (the correct conclusion to be drawn).

Confusing Attitude and Behavior

For any behavior questions such as, "Are you going to join COPE next week?", you do not have actual measures of behavior, but only self-reports that are subject to memory effects and to biases due to social desirability. For example, no matter how the question is worded, most surveys have around 5–10% overreporting of voter turnout.

Ignoring the Context

Ignoring the context is another broad category of mistakes made in analyzing polling results. At best, polling results are valid measures of attitudes at a specific point in time. In analyzing those results, you should be aware of the prevailing political and social atmosphere at the time of interviewing and be alert to anything that may have happened before, during, or after your poll that would be expected to influence your results. For example, if shortly before or during your poll there were a series of murders in which the bodies of the victims were wrapped in environmentalist literature, this would affect any question about COPE. Sometimes even the weather can play a role, as in a question about the biggest problem facing the state or nation today. Flooding might well be a significant answer in the aftermath of a flood but might never be mentioned any other time.

Important note: As part of the context of the poll, remember what population you sampled and do not generalize your results to a different population without at least noting why you think such a conclusion is correct. If you are only calling women, for example, you have no way of knowing whether the results hold true for men.

Erroneous Theories

The last category of mistakes made in analyzing polling data occurs when a poll is based on erroneous theories. For example, if you incorrectly believe that a person's reaction to COPE is directly related to support for Saudi Arabia, your analysis may be colored.

The relationship might be explained with wrong variables because you have not tested for spurious relationships or have ignored intervening relationships. In other words, there might really be a relationship between those two attitudes, but it probably has to do with some third factor that your poll might not cover. In this case, your poll would lack the questions you would need to judge between plausible alternative explanations for your results.

BEYOND THE BASIC ANALYSIS

Once you have gone to the effort and expense of doing a scientific poll, you probably want more than just the obvious conclusions drawn from a basic analysis. If you have past polling data, you will want to see how your results compare with past results. Within your own poll, you will want to look at what patterns occur, what opinions appear to be related, which subgroups believe and do what, and what clues you have for why people hold certain attitudes. But how do we explore those things?

In exploring relationships, you first need to distinguish dependent variables from independent variables. An **independent variable** is not affected by any of the other factors in your poll. A person's sex, profession, and age are independent variables — they will remain the same regardless of other factors.

A **dependent variable** might be caused or influenced by something else. For example, a person's attitude toward COPE is a dependent variable. That attitude depends on whether the individual is male or female, old or young, and so forth. When POLL-START (the software designed to complement this book) is used to run a cross tabulation, the independent variable (such as sex) must be at the top of the chart and the dependent variable (such as opinion) at the side. For example, we want to know that 14% of women polled are negative toward COPE.

If we reversed the independent and dependent variables, the computer would give us the useless information that 44% of those who are negative toward COPE are women. This information is meaningless because perhaps 44% of all the people interviewed are women.

To give another example, suppose you are looking at the relationship between the type of vehicle hitting pedestrians and the magnitude of the accident. Obviously, the magnitude of the accident depends on the type of vehicle; therefore, the vehicle is the independent variable, and the magnitude of the accident is the dependent variable. The computer would then give you a cross tabulation showing that 10% of pedestrian hit-and-run accidents involving a car end in fatalities, but 80% of pedestrian hit-and-run accidents involving a truck end in fatalities. This is a meaningful conclusion from a correctly percentaged analysis (with the type of vehicle at the top of the cross-tabulation chart, and the magnitude of the accident down the side).

If you had confused the variables and had magnitude at the top of the chart and type of vehicle down the side, you would have been told that 75% of pedestrian fatalities involve a car, but only 25% involve a truck. From that information you might conclude that trucks are safer for pedestrians. Obviously, however, that is false — a proper analysis shows that trucks are far more dangerous for pedestrians than cars, even though many more accidents involve cars than trucks.

But how do you explore the less-obvious relationships in a poll? Exploring such relationships takes common sense and perception. It is done by comparing cross tabulations to discover which relationships are significant. For example, you may discover that union members are far more favorable toward COPE than nonunion members, and men are more favorable than women. Both of those findings would be important to a membership drive. But are men more supportive because a higher percentage of men are union members? Or are union members more supportive because they have a greater percentage of men? Or are both related to some third variable?

A poll can never prove a relationship, but you could check by running a cross tabulation involving only male union members. Is that group more favorable toward COPE than men at large? If so, it would be reasonable to assume that union membership itself had some effect on positive feelings toward COPE. But if the male union members were no more favorable than all men, you might assume that the high ratings by union members were related to the fact that most union members are male.

Because human behavior is so complex, it is unlikely that you will be able to isolate one variable that is more important than all the others. Rather, you will get a range of educated guesses as to why people believe or behave in a certain way. For your group to make intelligent decisions based on educated guesses, you must be careful that your conclusions are based on statistically meaningful numbers and not due to sampling error or some bias in the polling procedure.

BEYOND ADVANCED ANALYSIS—OTHER TYPES OF STATISTICS

If your group has access to a person trained in statistics, there may be other uses for statistical data in addition to percentages. The bibliography to this book lists some resources that could be helpful in matching the appropriate statistical analysis with the kind of analysis needed and the nature of the data. Those topics are beyond the scope of this book and associated computer software.

Two types of statistics, other than percentages, are used most often. **Summary statistics,** such as means and standard deviations on single questions, allow you to summarize and compare where people's opinions concentrate and determine how much variety there is in those opinions. Other statistics give **measures of association,** such as correlations, that reveal how well knowing a respondent's answer to one question will enable you to predict his or her response to a second question.

CHECKLIST—ANALYZING THE RESULTS

1. Did you plan out your analysis before you conducted the poll?
2. Have you determined which are your independent and dependent variables?
3. Are your relationships really significant?
4. Have you overanalyzed your results?
5. Have you distinguished causality and association?
6. Have you looked at variations in respondent's opinions by relevant subgroups?
7. Have you considered the use of other types of statistics appropriate to the form of the data you have for each question?
8. Have you considered the context of your interviewing period and thus of your results?

CHAPTER TEN

Shortcuts and Pitfalls

Although there are efficient ways to conduct a poll, many popular shortcuts are really pitfalls. Throughout this book, we have suggested the easiest and most efficient ways to accomplish the various parts of a survey. In this chapter, we concentrate on the possible pitfalls. This chapter also will help you to critique and shop for polls.

WHAT IS ERROR?

There are two basic kinds of error in polling: random error and bias. **Random error** involves nonsystematic variation in results, whereas **bias** systematically influences results in one direction or another. Throughout this book, we have discussed sources of random error and bias and ways to cut down on each. Error can be associated with:

- ☐ The method of the interview
- ☐ The question content
- ☐ The interviewing
- ☐ The sampling
- ☐ The coverage of respondents
- ☐ The characteristics of the interviewer
- ☐ The analysis
- ☐ The processing of the survey

The biggest problem with surveys is that most error (other than sampling error) cannot be measured accurately, which means there is no way of knowing how much the results have been contaminated.

Bias is related to similar factors, particularly sampling, coverage of respondents, and question wording.

By heeding the alerts in this chapter and incorporating them into your planning, you should be able to avoid some of the biggest pitfalls in polling.

WHAT ARE THE MISTAKES TO AVOID?

Getting Started

Unfortunately, many polls get off to a bad start by:

- ☐ Including questions of interest that do not contribute to a cohesive survey or to the objectives of the survey.
- ☐ Doing insufficient thinking and planning on what you need to know to be able to use the polling information and understand the relationships observed in the poll results.
- ☐ Choosing a convenient population rather than the correct population for making inferences from your polling data.
- ☐ Generalizing your results to an incorrect or larger population than you actually sampled. For example, findings from a sample of registered voters should not be generalized to the entire population or to the actual voters in any election.
- ☐ Failing to plan the entire polling process adequately.
- ☐ Keeping insufficient records of the sample and the interviews during the survey.
- ☐ Underestimating the amount of time and work required in polling.
- ☐ Mixing polling and canvassing tasks. For example, political groups may try to add name recognition and persuasion techniques on to a poll. Polls are not the best way to do these tasks, and survey results are often invalidated in the process.
- ☐ Falling into the common pitfalls associated with any volunteer effort, including insufficient training, inadequate follow-up, insufficient rewards, and unrealistic demands.

Questionnaire Design and Wording

The most common mistakes in writing questions for public interest polls are:

- ☐ Failing to define enough independent variables (see Chapter 9 on Analysis) or questions that help you determine who believes what and why.
- ☐ Writing unbalanced questions (questions that present only one side of the issue).
- ☐ Excluding "no opinion" filters or "don't know" options in the belief that by so doing you can force respondents to give opinions (in actuality, you may force what does not exist).
- ☐ Including complex and technical questions that demand too much from respondents. Poor writing often systematically affects certain kinds of respondents such as those who have less interest and education.
- ☐ Paying too little attention to how each question acts as a context for understanding and responding to the next.
- ☐ Shortcutting the pretest in an effort to make up time, especially when the poll is running behind schedule.
- ☐ Overlooking the needs of the interviewers and coders in questionnaire design.

Interviewing

Some common pitfalls in interviewing are:

- ☐ Inadequate and superficial training for interviewers.
- ☐ Neglecting to edit the first interviews of every interviewer to catch errors early.
- ☐ Not continually recruiting and training replacement interviewers as good ones burn-out and volunteers drop out.
- ☐ Ignoring refusal conversions and follow-up on nonworking numbers because they are difficult and time consuming. This leaves surveys, especially volunteer surveys, with dangerously high refusal rates and low overall response rates.
- ☐ Ignoring call-backs or interviewing only during the evenings. This biases your sample by including a preponderance of people who are easy to reach.

Sampling

The most common pitfalls in sampling are:

☐ Choosing an easy sample (for example, whoever answers the phone) rather than insisting on the correct probability sample (for example, the named registered voter chosen in your sample).

☐ Improper use of replacement interviews. If you have drawn an oversample to compensate for nonresponse, you must attempt to interview the entire sample even if your goal has been reached. You should also not turn too early to replacements. Otherwise, you may be systematically undersampling certain kinds of people.

☐ Sampling from "dirty lists" or lists that contain duplicate listings. Dirty lists are lists with incorrect or out-of-date information.

 Data Processing

Common pitfalls in data processing are:

☐ Inadequate training and supervision of coders. Failing to check coders' work can result in inconsistencies in coding.

☐ Ignoring wild codes, invalid codes, and inconsistencies in data under the assumption that they are random errors. In fact, they may indicate that an entire questionnaire or series of questionnaires has been entered incorrectly.

☐ Trying to save time by not "cleaning" or verifying data.

 **Data Analysis**

Common pitfalls in data analysis include:

☐ Drawing unwarranted and unfounded conclusions from data.

☐ Assuming that the association of two concepts indicates causality, or a cause-and-effect relationship between the two, when that may not be the case.

☐ Inadequate anticipation of your data analysis needs in the planning phases of the poll. Careful focusing before the survey is taken helps you know what objectives and hypotheses you are testing and thus will need to analyze.

WHERE DO YOU GO FOR HELP?

You may want to enlist experts to check aspects of your poll, especially if you are relying heavily on volunteers. These checks are particularly important in questionnaire design, sampling, and data analysis which are the most technical and scientific parts of polling. Help often is readily available if you know where to look for it.

Colleges and universities are good sources of free assistance. Professors, graduate students, and student interns in statistics, business, natural resources, and social science departments frequently have interests and expertise in polling.

State and federal government research and information bureaus often have statisticians familiar with survey data. Political organizations, national interest groups, and labor unions often have access to regional or national staff with survey experience.

Media reporters increasingly are becoming familiar with surveys in their own work. Finally, large companies such as insurance companies and investment firms, often have statisticians on staff.

WHAT TO LOOK FOR IN EXPERTS

Any expert who advises you should have experience in the area you need help in, as well as general background experience in surveys. The following is a list of specifics to watch for in advisers:

☐ Expertise in your particular problem area. For example, a statistician could give you good advice on sampling but little help with wording questions.
☐ Appreciation for what it means to work with volunteers and knowledge of the particular needs and problems this presents (particularly in planning, interviewing, and questionnaire construction).
☐ Familiarity with your organization's issues, goals, and resources.

Polling is a careful science and art. It is a tool well within the grasp of public interest groups but only with careful planning and understanding of the range of methods and issues involved.

Important note: One disadvantage of having so many people available with some experience in polling is that they all
consider themselves "experts" in this "easy and intuitive"
task. Choose your experts carefully and plan early where and when
you will need their help.

HOW TO CUT COSTS

Most public interest groups can get the needed resources for a poll
from within the organization or from supporters. You should know,
however, that using these resources and relying on volunteers can
increase costs in other ways: in person power, time, fatigue, and
frustration. The resources you use for your poll must be evaluated in
terms of what is available to your organization and what are the
hidden costs (for example, using volunteers instead of paid
interviewers).

Piggybacking questions of other public interest groups in your
poll can spread costs among your groups. We advise, however, that
one group take ultimate responsibility for the poll.

One of the best ways to cut costs is to plan ahead to avoid
mistakes. Other factors also can be manipulated to cut
costs, such as:

- ☐ Shorter questionnaire length
- ☐ Smaller sample size
- ☐ Deleting open-ended questions
- ☐ Using answer sheets instead of questionnaires for every
  interview
- ☐ Entering data into the computer directly from
  questionnaires
- ☐ Sampling from existing lists (especially lists like registered
  voters lists).

Remember that all of these cost-cutting measures have tradeoffs
that will be more or less acceptable depending on the objectives of
your survey.

One last aid in controlling costs is to anticipate when cash may be
required. The following checklist outlines for you the most frequent
items in a survey that actually cost money. The assumption is that
design, implementation, training, and sampling are being done by
existing staff and volunteers.

CHECKLIST—COSTS INVOLVED IN CONDUCTING A SURVEY

For the questionnaire:
1. Typing the original and revised forms
2. Photocopying (preferably enough copies for all interviews)
3. Assembling the questionnaires

For interviewing:
1. Telephones (installation and rate charges)
2. Supervisors for each telephone facility
3. Paid interviewers
4. Training materials for interviewers (typing and photocopying)
5. Typing and photocopying pretest evaluation forms
6. Refusal conversion calls (you may want paid staff)
7. Operator assistance calls to verify new and nonworking numbers
8. Verification calls

For the sample:
1. Buying the list
2. Typing and photocopying the coversheets
3. Clerical time to transfer the sample to coversheets

For the analysis:
1. Salaries for coders, keypunchers, or other data entry personnel
2. Computer time
3. Programmer time to clean data and build the dataset
4. Report typing and photocopying

Annotated Bibliography

Babbie, Earl R. *Survey Research Methods*. Belmont, CA: Wadsworth, 1973. General overview to polling. Good basic textbook.

Backstrom, Charles H., and Gerald Hursh-Cesar. *Survey Research*, 2d ed. New York: John Wiley & Sons, 1981. A good basic overview to polling. Especially good sections on question wording and questionnaire layout.

Belson, William A. *The Design and Understanding of Survey Questions*. England: Gower Publishers, 1981. Presents research on respondents' understanding of common questions.

Bishop, George F., Robert W. Oldendich, and Alfred J. Tuchfarber. *Effects of Presenting One Versus Two Sides*. Paper presented at American Public Opinion Research Meetings, 1983. Good discussion of the impact of the interviewer, method of interviewing, and questionnaire design on responses.

Bradburn, Norman M., and Seymour Sudman. *Improving Interview Method and Questionnaire Design*. San Francisco: Jossey-Bass Publishers, 1979. A good overview to polling. Includes the mechanics of setting up a questionnaire and a simplified discussion of some of the newer techniques.

Cannell, Charles F., et al. "Research on Interviewing Techniques". *Sociological Methodology* 4 (1981): 389-437. Presents research on improving response quality with better probing, reinforcement, and commitment from respondents.

Converse, Jean. *Conversations at Random*. New York: John Wiley & Sons, Inc., 1974. Human anecdotes on interviewing.

Dillman, Don A. *Mail and Telephone Surveys: The Total Design Method*. New York: John Wiley & Sons, Inc., 1978. An overview and good discussion of administering telephone surveys. Good overview of general sampling techniques.

Ferber, Robert, et al. *What Is a Survey?* Washington, DC: American Statistical Association, 1980. Good general overview to polling.

Frey, James H. *Survey Research by Telephone*. Beverly Hills, CA: Sage Publications, 1973. Good general overview to polling.

Groves, Robert M., and Robert L. Kahn. *Surveys by Telephone: A National Comparison With Personal Interviews*. New York: Academic Press, 1979. Good analysis of how the interview method affects responses to questions. Useful comparison of coverage in telephone and personal surveys.

Kalton, Graham. *Introduction to Survey Sampling*, Beverly Hills, CA: Sage Publications, 1983. Introduction to and overview of sampling theory.

Kish, Leslie. *Survey Sampling*, New York: John Wiley & Sons, Inc., 1965. The classic text on sampling theories and procedures, including within-household selection by full household listing.

Moser, Sir Claus, and G. Kalton. *Survey Methods in Social Investigation*. New York: Basic Books, Inc., 1974. A general text about survey methods that is particularly strong in its chapter on sampling and also has good material on interviewing and analysis.

Payne, Stanley L. *The Art of Asking Questions*. Princeton, NJ: Princeton University Press, 1951. A very readable, entertaining classic, which is still largely accurate.

Roll, Charles W., Jr., and Albert H. Cantril. *Polls: Their Use and Misuse in Politics*. New York: Basic Books, Inc., 1972. A good guide to possible errors in interpretation.

Schuman, Howard, and Stanley Presser. "Question Wording as an Independent Variable in Survey Analysis." *Sociological Methods and Research* 612 (1977): 151-170. Summary of new research on question wording problems.

Schuman, Howard, and Stanley Presser. *Questions and Answers in Attitude Surveys*. New York: Academic Press, 1981. Complete and detailed analysis of the newest research question-wording and question-order effects, with added insights into what causes such effects and which respondents are most susceptible.

Sudman, S., and N. Bradburn. *Response Effects in Surveys*. Chicago: Aldine, 1974. An overview of response effects in interviewing.

Sudman, Seymour, et al. "Modest Expectations — the Effects of Interviewers' Prior Expectations on Responses." *Sociological Methods and Research* 6(2) (1977): 171-182. Discusses the impact of interviewers' beliefs on responses.

Survey Research Center. *Interviewers' Manual*. Ann Arbor, MI: University of Michigan Institute for Social Research, 1983. A step-by-step guide to interviewing, with handouts for training interviewers.

Trodahl, V. C., and R. E. Carter, "Random Selection of Respondents with Households in Phone Surveys," *Journal of Marketing Research* 1

(1964): 71–76. Discusses respondent selection within households using an alternative method to full household listing.

Waksberg, J. "Sampling Methods for Random Digit Dialing," *Journal of the American Statistical Association* (1978) 73:40–46. Describes a method for generating a random digit dialing sample that cuts down on the number of nonworking numbers by sampling in two stages.

Weisberg, Herbert, and Bruce D. Bowen. *An Introduction to Survey Research and Data Analysis*. San Francisco: W.H. Freeman Co., 1977. A good discussion of basic analysis and statistics, with special attention to what statistics are appropriate for what kind of data. Also a good discussion of coding variables.

Modified Trodahl/Carter Method

Six versions of the respondent-selection key to be used with the modified Trodahl/Carter method within-household sampling follow.* See Chapter 7 for a detailed discussion of the method.

Version 1 (as marked by interviewer)

	Number of Adults in Housing Unit			
	1 Adult	2 Adults	3 Adults	4 or more
0 Women	Adult 01	Oldest Man 03	Oldest Man 06	Youngest Man 10
1 Woman	Adult 02	Man 04	Youngest Man 07	Woman 11
2 Women		Youngest Woman 05	Youngest Woman 08	Youngest Man 12
3 Women			Oldest Woman 09	Man or Youngest Man 13
4 Women				Youngest Woman 14

Number of Women (vertical axis label)

*Reprinted with permission of Macmillan Publishing Company from *Survey Research*, 2d ed. by Charles H. Backstrom and Gerald Hursh-Cesar. New York: Macmillan Publishing Company, 1981.

Version 2

Number of Adults in Housing Unit

	1 Adult	2 Adults	3 Adults	4 or more
0 Women	Adult 01	Oldest Man 03	Youngest Man 06	Youngest Man 10
1 Woman	Adult 02	Woman 04	Woman 07	Oldest Man 11
2 Women		Oldest Woman 05	Youngest Woman 08	Youngest Woman 12
3 Women			Youngest Woman 09	Oldest Woman 13
4 Women				Oldest Woman 14

Number of Women

Version 3

Number of Adults in Housing Unit

	1 Adult	2 Adults	3 Adults	4 or more
0 Women	Adult 01	Youngest Man 03	Youngest Man 06	Oldest Man 10
1 Woman	Adult 02	Woman 04	Oldest Man 07	Woman 11
2 Women		Oldest Woman 05	Man 08	Oldest Man 12
3 Women			Youngest Woman 09	Man or Oldest Man 13
4 Women				Oldest Woman 14

Number of Women

Version 4

Number of Adults in Housing Unit

	1 Adult	2 Adults	3 Adults	4 or more
0 Women	01 Adult	03 Youngest Man	06 Oldest Man	10 Oldest Man
1 Woman	02 Adult	04 Man	07 Woman	11 Youngest Man
2 Women		05 Youngest Woman	08 Oldest Woman	12 Oldest Woman
3 Women			09 Oldest Woman	13 Youngest Woman
4 Women				14 Youngest Woman

Number of Women (row axis label)

Version 5

Number of Adults in Housing Unit

	1 Adult	2 Adults	3 Adults	4 or more
0 Women	01 Adult	03 Oldest Man	06 Middle Man	10 2d Oldest Man
1 Woman	02 Adult	04 Woman	07 Youngest Man	11 Middle Man
2 Women		05 Youngest Woman	08 Oldest Woman	12 Oldest or Youngest Man
3 Women			09 Middle Woman	13 Middle Woman
4 Women				14 2d Youngest Woman

Number of Women (row axis label)

Version 6

Number of Adults in Housing Unit

		1 Adult	2 Adults	3 Adults	4 or more
	0 Women	01 Adult	03 Youngest Man	06 Middle Man	10 2d Oldest Man
	1 Woman	02 Adult	04 Man	07 Oldest Man	11 Middle Man
	2 Women		05 Oldest Woman	08 Man	12 Oldest or Youngest Woman
	3 Women			09 Middle Woman	13 Middle Woman
	4 Women				14 2d Oldest Woman

Number of Women (vertical axis label)

Sample Questionnaire and Poll Format

Important note: This appendix is designed to give you:

☐ Examples of several kinds of poll questions.

☐ A typical layout and progression of questions.

☐ Samples of conventions that are helpful to interviewers in skip questions and open-ended questions.

A word of caution: Be careful not to load your poll with too many questions. It can be a serious mistake to include lots of questions about things you'd like to know but don't necessarily need to know for survey purposes.

SAMPLE POLL QUESTIONS AND FORMAT

Lead-in

LEAD-IN OR WARM-UP

Hello, is _____ (VOTER'S NAME) there?

Hello, I'm _____ (YOUR NAME) from Public Opinion Research Surveys. Your name was randomly selected from a sample of registered voters. We would like to take a few minutes of your time to talk to you about issues and local affairs in Atlantis. Your answers will be kept strictly confidential.

Questions

Q1. Generally speaking, what do you think is the most important problem facing our state today? **Q2.** Anything else? (REMEMBER, DON'T READ THE RESPONSES) (WRITE AND CHECK CODE)

    Q1. First mention _____

    Q2. Second mention _____

    (CODED AS QUESTION 2)

	FIRST MENTION	SECOND MENTION
OPEN-ENDED QUES-TIONS	○ 1.1 ECONOMY __ (GO TO Q3)_____	○ 2.1
	○ 1.2 ENVIRONMENT__(GO TO Q4)	○ 2.2
	○ 1.3 AGRICULTURE __ (GO TO Q4)	○ 2.3
	○ 1.4 OTHER: SPECIFY:_____ (GO TO Q4)	○ 2.4
	○ 1.5 DON'T KNOW __ (GO TO Q4)	○ 2.5
	○ 1.9-MISSING (NA–not ascertained or no second response given)	○ 2.9

(IF "ECONOMY" IS NOT MENTIONED IN Q1 OR Q2, GO TO Q4)

SKIP-PATTERN QUESTION

Q3. IF ANSWER IS "ECONOMY" FOR EITHER QUESTION, PROBE: What part of the economy do you think is the biggest problem for us now? (WRITE AND CHECK CODE)

○ 3.1 JOBS (UNEMPLOYMENT) ○ 3.6 INFLATION
○ 3.2 INTEREST RATES ○ 3.7 OTHER:
○ 3.3 RECESSION (SPECIFY)
○ 3.4 BUDGET DEFICIT ○
○ 3.5 TAXATION _____
○ 3.8 DON'T KNOW
3.9-MISSING
(INAP-skipped)

OPEN-ENDED QUESTION

Q4. Which part of your household budget was most hurt by the recession in 1982? What necessities were hardest to buy or had to be cut from your budget? (TAKE DOWN ANSWER VERBATIM) _____

Q5. Now we would like to know how people feel about an income tax break for school tuition. Parents who send their children to private and parochial schools must pay tuition. Would you *favor* or *oppose* giving parents a break in their income tax for tuition to private and parochial schools, or haven't you thought much about it?

- ○ 5.1 FAVOR (GO TO Q 6)
- ○ 5.2 OPPOSE (GO TO Q 7)
- ○ 5.3 DON'T KNOW, HAVEN'T THOUGHT MUCH ABOUT IT (GO TO Q7)
- ○ 5.9-MISSING

Q6. Would you *favor* an income tax break for tuition even if it reduced the money available for public schools?

- ○ 6.1 YES
- ○ 6.2 NO
- ○ 6.3 DON'T KNOW
- ○ 6.9-MISSING (INCLUDES CORRECTLY SKIPPED)

GRADED RESPONSE

Q7. Some people think that Atlantis' current environmental regulations hinder economic growth in our state a great deal. Others think these laws affect economic growth slightly, if at all. Do you think that our current environmental regulations *hinder* economic growth *a great deal, somewhat, only slightly,* or *not at all,* or *haven't you thought much about this?*

- ○ 7.1 A GREAT DEAL
- ○ 7.2 SOMEWHAT
- ○ 7.3 ONLY SLIGHTLY
- ○ 7.4 NOT AT ALL
- ○ 7.5 HELPS ECONOMY GROW (VOLUNTEERED)
- ○ 7.6 DON'T KNOW
- ○ 7.7 HAVEN'T THOUGHT MUCH ABOUT IT
- ○ 7.9-MISSING

ISSUE OPINION

Q8. Recently there has been discussion about whether or not gender should be a factor in setting insurance rates. Do you *favor* or *oppose* the use of the gender of the applicant (whether the person is male or female) as a way to set insurance rates?

- ○ 8.1 FAVOR
- ○ 8.2 OPPOSE
- ○ 8.3 DON'T KNOW
- ○ 8.9-MISSING

SPECIFIC
SOURCE
OF INFOR-
MATION

Q9. Where would you say you have received most of your information on the issue of gender and insurance rates: from television, from radio, from newspapers, from word of mouth through friends, from direct mail, from your insurance agent, or from some other source?

- O 9.1 TELEVISION
- O 9.2 RADIO
- O 9.3 NEWSPAPERS/MAGAZINES
- O 9.4 WORD OF MOUTH THROUGH FRIENDS
- O 9.5 DIRECT MAIL
- O 9.6 FROM INSURANCE AGENT
- O 9.7 OTHER (PLEASE SPECIFY): _____
- O 9.8 DON'T KNOW
- O 9.9 MISSING

POLITICAL
JOB
RATING

Q10. In general, how good a job would you say the State Legislature is doing in solving our economic problems? Is it doing an *excellent* job, a *good* job, a *fair* job, or a *poor* job?

- O 10.1 EXCELLENT
- O 10.2 GOOD
- O 10.3 FAIR
- O 10.4 POOR
- O 10.5 NOT SURE
- O 10.9-MISSING

Q11–16. Now I'd like to get your feelings toward some political groups in our state. You'll rate these groups on something we call a "feeling thermometer," and here's how it works:

FEELING THERMOM-ETER

I'll read the name of a group and I'll ask you to rate that group using a thermometer that runs from 0 degrees (very cool) to 100 degrees (very warm). On this thermometer, ratings between 50 and 100 degrees mean you feel favorable and warm toward that group. Ratings between 0 and 50 degrees mean you don't feel too favorable toward that group. If you don't feel particularly warm or cool, you would rate that group at the 50-degree mark (or neutral). If you don't know the group, just tell me and we'll move on. (PAUSE)

Now, on this scale, which runs from 0 degrees (very cool) to 100 degrees (very warm), how would you rate your feelings toward (READ THE NAME OF EACH GROUP AND RECORD THE ACTUAL RATING ANSWERED. CODE RATINGS OF 96 OR ABOVE AS 96.)

```
   −           − / +          +
   0            50           100
```

	Actual Rating	Don't Know -97	Don't Recognize -98	Missing -99
11. Business people				
12. Farmers/ranchers				
13. Environmentalists				
14. Labor unions				
15. Teachers				
16. Women's groups				

(REMEMBER: ALL RATINGS ABOVE 96 RECEIVE A "96" CODE)

ISSUE
AWARE-
NESS

Q17. An issue of public concern in our state is the new waste-water disposal policy being considered by the Legislature. Would you say that this issue is of *great concern, moderate concern, slight concern,* or *no concern at all* to you, or haven't you heard much about it?

    O 17.1 GREAT CONCERN _____

    O 17.2 MODERATE CONCERN _____

    O 17.3 SLIGHT CONCERN _____

    O 17.4 NO CONCERN AT ALL _____

    O 17.5 DON'T KNOW __ (GO TO Q22)

    O 17.6 HAVEN'T THOUGHT MUCH ABOUT IT __ (GO TO Q22)

    O 17.9–MISSING

NAME
RECOG-
NITION
AND
APPROVAL

Q18–21. Several groups have been active in this waste-water disposal issue. I'll read you a list of groups, and I'd like you to tell me if you *approve strongly, approve, disapprove,* or *disapprove strongly* of the position each has taken on this issue. If you don't recognize the group or don't know much about its position, just let me know and we'll move on. (READ NAMES OF GROUPS IN GRID)

	Approve Strongly (.1)	Approve (.2)	Dis-approve (.3)	Dis-approve Strongly (.4)	Don't Know (.6)	Don't Recog. Name (.7)	Missing (-9)
18. City Council							
19. Coalition to Protect the Envir-orment							
20. Ranchers Inc.							
21. Keep It Clean							

SKIP-
PATTERN
QUESTION

Q22. Regardless of how you may vote in a particular election, do you generally consider yourself to be a Democrat, a Republican, or what?

    ○ 22.1 DEMOCRAT __ (GO TO Q24)
    ○ 22.2 REPUBLICAN __ (GO TO Q24)
    ○ 22.3 INDEPENDENT __ (GO TO Q23) _____
    ○ 22.4 DON'T KNOW __ (GO TO Q23) _____
    ○ 22.5 REFUSED __ (GO TO Q24)
    ○ 22.9-MISSING

PARTY
PREFER-
ENCE

Q22 & Q23
CAN BE
CODED TO
ONE

Q23. Do you generally consider yourself to be closer to the Democratic or the Republican Party?

    ○ 23.1 DEMOCRATIC
    ○ 23.2 REPUBLICAN
    ○ 23.3 NEITHER (INDEPENDENT)
    ○ 23.4 STILL DON'T KNOW
    ○ 23.5 REFUSED
    ○ 23.9-MISSING (AND CORRECTLY SKIPPED)

There are just a few questions remaining now for statistical purposes:

INFORMA-
TION
SOURCE

Q24. When it comes to receiving information on local current events, which information source do you rely on the most: *television, local newspapers, radio,* or *another source?*

    ○ 24.1 TELEVISION
    ○ 24.2 LOCAL NEWSPAPERS
    ○ 24.3 RADIO
    ○ 24.4 OTHER (PLEASE SPECIFY): _____
    ○ 24.5 DON'T KNOW
    ○ 24.9-MISSING

DEMO-
GRAPHICS

Q25. What is the highest level of education you have completed, *grade school, high school,* or college?

    ○ 25.1 GRADE SCHOOL
    ○ 25.2 HIGH SCHOOL
    ○ 25.3 COLLEGE (INCLUDES JUNIOR COLLEGE AND ASSOCIATE DEGREE)
    ○ 25.4 REFUSED
    ○ 25.9-MISSING

Q26. In what year were you born? _____ (TAKE DOWN YEAR AND CODE)

- O 26.1 18–24 years
- O 26.2 25–34
- O 26.3 35–44
- O 26.4 45–54
- O 26.5 55–64
- O 26.6 Over 65
- O 26.7 REFUSED
- O 26.9–MISSING

Q27. What is your occupation? _____ (IF NOT OBVIOUS TO YOU, ASK: What business or industry is that?) __ (DO NOT READ CATEGORIES – RECORD ANSWERS IN BLANK AND STAFF WILL CODE LATER.)

- O 27.1 PROFESSIONAL (DOCTOR, ATTORNEY, TEACHER)
- O 27.2 WHITE COLLAR (MANAGEMENT, SMALL BUSINESS, SALES)
- O 27.3 BLUE COLLAR (AND TRADE UNIONISTS)
- O 27.4 CLERICAL/OFFICE/TECHNICIAN
- O 27.5 FARMER/RANCHER
- O 27.6 RETIRED
- O 27.7 HOMEMAKER/DAYCARE GIVER
- O 27.8 STUDENT
- O 27.9 OTHER
- O 27.99–MISSING

Q28. Finally, for statistical purposes only, I am going to read you a series of income categories. Just tell me the *number* of the category that includes the income, before taxes were taken out, of all members of your family who were living at home during 1984. This figure includes dividends, interest, salaries, wages, pensions, and all other income of the family (IF UNCERTAIN, ASK: What would be your best guess?) (READ THESE CATEGORIES, INCLUDING THE CATEGORY NUMBER.)

- ○ 28.1 Less than $6000
- ○ 28.2 $6,000–15,000
- ○ 28.3 $15,000–25,000
- ○ 28.4 $25,000–40,000
- ○ 28.5 $40,000–60,000
- ○ 28.6 Over $60,000
- ○ 28.7 REFUSED
- ○ 28.8 DON'T KNOW (DON'T READ)
- ○ 28.9–MISSING

This completes our interview. Thank you so much for your help and for your time in completing our survey. Good night, and thank you again.

| QUESTIONS TO BE CODED BY INTERVIEWER AFTER COMPLETION OF SURVEY: |

Q29. Sex:
- ○ 29.1 Male
- ○ 29.2 Female
- ○ 29.9 Uncertain

SELF-
CODED,
LATER

Q30. County:
- ○ 30.1 Davidson Co.
- ○ 30.2 Brookshire Co.
- ○ 30.3 Craftsman Co.
- ○ 30.4 Proud Co.
- ○ 30.9–MISSING

Q31. State Legislative District: _____ (From registered voters list)

- ○ 31.1 HD #1
- ○ 31.2 HD #2
- ○ 31.3 HD #3
- ○ 31.4 HD #4
- ○ 31.5 HD #5
- ○ 31.6 HD #6
- ○ 31.9-MISSING

Sample Hand-Tabulation Grid

Q1. Gender:

	Male	Female
		/

Q2. Party Identification:

	Republican	Independent Don't Know	Democrat
	/		

Q3 Vote:

	Jack	Jill	Undecided
		/	

Vote by Party Identification and Gender:

	Jack	Jill	Undecided
Republican		**/**	
Independent			
Democrat			

Male			
Female		**/**	

Gender impact on vote controlling for party identification:

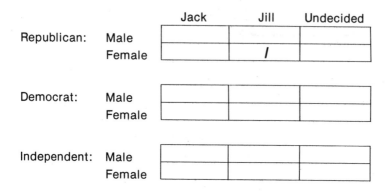

This questionnaire is designed to evaluate Jack's and Jill's support in an upcoming election by party identification and gender. For each questionnaire, a mark is entered in the appropriate boxes of the grid corresponding to the respondent's answers. Thus, a female Republican voting for Jill would be coded as indicated in the grid by the /. The first part of the grid reveals the distributions for each question. The middle part shows candidate support by gender and party identification. The last part of the grid shows whether gender made any difference in support of the two candidates once party identification was controlled.

Sample Cross Tabulations from
POLLSTART

The following tables are examples of cross tabulations and frequency tables produced through the POLLSTART software package. The first cross tabulation, entitled "How People Favoring Higher Drinking Age Feel About Curfew," was produced with the command:

A>report qa filename responses file row 2 col 4

The second table, the frequency table of the raw data from the survey, was produced with the command:

A>report raw qa file responses file

Legislative District Poll 10/84 — How People Favoring Higher Drinking Age Feel About Curfew

	TOTALS	4.1 Yes 100%/157	4.2 No 100%/114	4.3 Undecided 100%/37	4.9 Missing Data 100%/3
2.1 Yes	72%/223	80%/125	58%/66	78%/29	100%/3
2.2 No	23%/71	17%/27	36%/41	8%/3	0%/0
2.3 Undecided	5%/17	3%/5	6%/7	14%/5	0%/0
2.9 Missing data	/0	/1	/3	/1	/0

Note: Question 2 (rows) asked: Should the drinking age be raised to 21? YES–NO–UNDECIDED
Question 4 (columns) asked: Do you favor a driving curfew? YES–NO–UNDECIDED

Frequency Table for Legislative District Poll 10/84

Q1:		total	n = 310	Lottery?
	1:	47%	n = 145	yes
	2:	41%	n = 128	no
	3:	12%	n = 37	undecided
	9:	miss	n = 6	missing data
Q2:		total	n = 311	Raise drinking age to 21?
	1:	72%	n = 223	yes
	2:	23%	n = 71	no
	3:	5%	n = 17	undecided
	9:	miss	n = 5	missing data
Q3:		total	n = 308	Legislative priority of containing health care cost?
	1:	68%	n = 210	high priority
	2:	19%	n = 60	medium priority
	3:	8%	n = 25	low priority
	4:	4%	n = 13	undecided
	9:	miss	n = 8	missing data
Q4:		total	n = 313	Driving curfew?
	1:	50%	n = 158	yes
	2:	37%	n = 117	no
	3:	12%	n = 38	undecided
	9:	miss	n = 3	missing data
Q5:		total	n = 312	Teacher tenure
	1:	18%	n = 55	eliminated
	2:	12%	n = 38	retained
	3:	63%	n = 198	modified
	4:	7%	n = 21	undecided
	9:	miss	n = 4	missing data
Q6:		total	n = 310	Severance tax?
	1:	14%	n = 44	too high
	2:	6%	n = 18	too low
	3:	64%	n = 197	about right
	4:	16%	n = 51	undecided
	9:	miss	n = 6	missing data
Q7:		total	n = 316	Nonsmoking areas in restaurants?
	1:	79%	n = 251	yes
	2:	16%	n = 51	no
	3:	4%	n = 14	undecided
	9:	miss	n = 0	missing data
Q8:		total	n = 311	Increase penalties on delinquent property taxes?
	1:	76%	n = 236	yes
	2:	12%	n = 36	no
	3:	13%	n = 39	undecided
	9:	miss	n = 5	missing data
Q9:		total	n = 313	School funding?
	1:	49%	n = 152	increased
	2:	4%	n = 12	decreased

3:	41%	n =	129	kept about the same
4:	6%	n =	20	undecided
9:	miss	n =	3	missing data
Q10:	total	n =	311	Cities and counties assess taxes?
1:	60%	n =	186	yes
2:	33%	n =	102	no
3:	7%	n =	23	undecided
9:	miss	n =	5	missing data
Q11:	total	n =	312	University funding?
1:	43%	n =	135	increased
2:	8%	n =	25	decreased
3:	44%	n =	137	kept about the same
4:	5%	n =	15	undecided
9:	miss	n =	4	missing data
Q12:	total	n =	265	Business/labor?
1:	14%	n =	36	pro-labor
2:	28%	n =	74	pro-business
3:	58%	n =	155	fair to both
9:	miss	n =	51	missing data
Q13:	total	n =	306	Legislative effort into economy and jobs?
1:	41%	n =	125	too little
2:	6%	n =	18	too much
3:	34%	n =	103	about right
4:	20%	n =	60	undecided
9:	miss	n =	10	missing data
Q14:	total	n =	313	Legislative effort to protect environment?
1:	43%	n =	136	too little
2:	8%	n =	25	too much
3:	42%	n =	133	about right
4:	6%	n =	19	undecided
9:	miss	n =	3	missing data

Frequency Table for Legislative District Poll 10/84 *(continued)*

Case Study

This appendix presents a brief sketch of a hypothetical organization considering a public opinion poll. This outline shows briefly, step by step, the entire "operation" of doing a poll.

Background: The Coalition to Protect the Environment (COPE) is a statewide group of volunteer activists on conservation issues. They have two goals for their organization during the coming year:

☐ To increase their membership
☐ To encourage action in support of a new wastewater disposal referendum.

COPE doesn't know how much support it has from the public, what the public recognition for their group or their issue is, or how the public feels about the new referendum.

The following is a list of the steps COPE should take in conducting a poll or survey to help them answer these questions. Answers should help them plan how to get more members and encourage the public to become active and supportive of the referendum.

 CHECKLIST—CONDUCTING A POLL

1. Decide to do a poll — determine it to be a statewide poll using a sample of 400 registered voters.
2. Secure the lists (voter registration lists) from which to draw the sample, being careful not to underestimate how much time and difficulty there can be in securing lists that are "clean" and free of duplication.

3. Pick a coordinator to find and secure a centralized telephone bank (minimum of five to ten telephones), recruit and train volunteers and substitutes for interviewing, telephone numbers searches, data entry, etc. Lead time for preparation is estimated at 4-6 weeks. Calculate the number of nights and shifts needed to complete the poll within 1 week.

4. Write the poll, which probably should be 10-15 minutes in length, including these types of questions: name recognition question for COPE, issue question on the proposal, feeling thermometer on groups and individuals prominent in the proposal campaign, information source question, gauge of willingness to work for the referendum, and demographics.

5. Run the poll design, sampling procedure, and questionnaire by several knowledgeable people for their reactions and suggestions.

6. Draw the sample; prepare the paperwork for the actual interviewing (photocopying calling lists, looking up telephone numbers, copying response sheets and grids, photocopying enough questionnaires, etc.). Allow at least 2 weeks.

7. Pretest the poll, using a pretest form. Don't neglect this step. Revise the questionnaire and reproduce response sheets and questionnaires.

8. Calculate the number of nights and shifts needed to complete the poll within 1 week. Finalize the schedule of volunteers and make sure there are a few substitutes for each shift. Brief interviewers the first night on the final questionnaire and procedures.

9. Conduct the poll, including appointments, call-backs, and some refusal conversions, if possible. Be sure to allot enough time. To complete a 10-minute survey of 400 people in 1 week, you will need six to eight telephones, with shifts Monday through Thursday nights and on weekends.

10. Clean the data. Edit completed questionnaires after each day's calling; get cleaned questionnaires to data entry people right away. Give feedback to interviewers on any errors they are making.

11. Begin data input as soon as possible so that cross tabulations can be pulled as soon as all questionnaires are entered. Run basic breaks or obvious cross tabulations.
12. Develop an analysis of results, rerunning any additional cross tabulations as needed. Share with knowledgeable people to help interpret results, content, strategies indicated, target populations, etc.
13. Organize a thank-you party for volunteers and send thank-you notes to contributors of telephones, etc.

Many of these tasks take place simultaneously. The flowchart of Figure 3-1 shows the layout of such a polling plan.

About POLLSTART

The book you have in your hand is designed to tell you everything you need to know to conduct a public opinion poll. However, if you have access to a personal or office computer, you may want to use it in conjunction with the software program POLLSTART. POLLSTART, its manual, and this handbook, used together, give you a complete package for polling from sampling through analysis.

POLLSTART, a computer program for office and home systems, tabulates and reports polling responses. POLLSTART can accommodate questionnaires of any length with unlimited numbers of responses. The only limitation is the capacity of your computer.

POLLSTART comes with a detailed, easy-to-use manual. It explains how to set up your questionnaire, enter data, and produce the reports you need. The program itself has a "Help" menu to get you through the learning stage.

POLLSTART generates reports that let you look at polling data from every possible angle. In addition to producing raw data reports, POLLSTART can cross-tabulate each question against all other questions. Multivariable cross tabulations are possible with the use of filters and make reporting possibilities practically endless.

Data entered on separate machines can be merged for reporting. This is a real convenience if you need results yesterday.

The latest version of POLLSTART is written for MS-DOS machines. POLLSTART is also available for CPM systems in an earlier version, which lacks some of the refined niceties but gets all the same work done. Both versions come with a manual.

POLLSTART was developed by Montana Alliance for Progressive Policy, which also offers occasional training seminars and provides back-up support for software users. For more information, contact MAPP, PO Box 961, Helena, MT 59624; phone 406-443-7283.

POLLSTART is available from Island Press. For information on price and availability, contact Island Press at PO Box 7, Covelo, CA 95428; phone 707-983-6432.

Glossary of Terms

acquiescence bias — term used to describe the tendency for respondents to agree with questions on which they don't have an opinion or which have certain formats.

balanced question — question in which both sides of an issue are presented with equal weight.

banner run — the cross-tabulation run of your attitude and behavior questions by your basic subgroups, usually your demographic variables.

bias — systematic over- or underrepresentation of certain kinds of people or answers.

break — a data analysis run.

call-back — the procedure where sample numbers are called again when there is initially no answer or a busy signal. Call-backs are done to increase the chances of having each sampled household fall in the completed sample.

central office code (COC) — the second set of three digits after the area code in a ten-digit telephone number. For example, in the number 313-763-1248, the "763" is the COC.

close-ended questions — questions where the respondent is provided with a set of possible responses to use in answering the question.

codebook — a guide to the dataset for each question. It includes all response categories and codes, indications of missing data, and variable numbers.

coding — assigning a numeric value to the verbal response to a survey question which categorizes that response.

confidence interval — the statistical odds that the real population value falls within a range around the survey estimate plus or minus the sampling error. The 95% confidence interval, which is the standard, says that 95% of the time we would be drawing the correct conclusion about the population values from the survey's measure of the values.

consistency checking — in data cleaning, checking for invalid or wild codes, codes that were not used for any answer in a question, or answers that are inconsistent with other answers.

contaminate — introducing error or bias into a task.

covariation — when two concepts covary, they change in tandem, for example, systematically increasing or decreasing in strength.

coverage — coverage refers to the completeness of your sample listing, that is, the degree to which your sampling frame truly includes all members of the population.

coversheet — the first page of the interview, which is used to keep track of the calls made, the result of the calls, the sample, and the household listing, if used.

crisscross, or **cross-reference directories** — directories that list people by telephone number or by address.

cross tabulations — bivariate frequency distributions that show at the same time the relationship between the responses to two questions. See **two-way tables.**

dataset — the computer file of the numeric coding and numeric identification of your interviews' responses.

demographics — basic social and political characteristics of respondents.

dependent variable — a factor that might be influenced by other factors (e.g., an individual's attitude toward something).

error — anything that changes the measurement of any concept such that the survey response is different from the true value in the population.

fixed interval sample (also known as **systematic sample**) — sampling, usually from a list, where you take a random start to select your first sampling unit and then systematically go a fixed interval down the list of the sampling frame to choose each additional sampling unit.

frequency distributions — lists of the number of respondents who gave each answer to each question.

household listing — the procedure in which the person who initially answers the telephone is asked to list the members of the household. From that listing the respondent is selected according to a set of procedures. In this case, household is defined as all people who reside permanently at the address called.

hypothesis — the statement of the relationship between two concepts as measured by questions in the survey.

independent variable — a factor not affected by any other factors (e.g., an individual's sex, profession, or age).

in-depth survey — 20-60 minute survey that assesses public opinion on one or more topics in depth.

interval of selection — interval between names drawn for a sample from a list. The interval is determined by dividing the total population size (i.e., size of the list) by the sample size.

interview number — a unique, sequential number on the interview and in the dataset for each completed survey questionnaire, used to identify the respondent or the interview.

intervening variables — concepts or conditions that come between the independent and dependent variables. Frequently, attitudes are the results of many interrelated factors, and these are the influences that truly account for the observed relationships.

interviewer variability (or **effects**) — the differences in responses depending on who does the interviewing.

loaded question — a question in which one answer is more likely to be chosen because it is clearly more prestigious, more socially desirable, or reflects the status quo.

measures of association — statistics that summarize the magnitude of the relationship between two variables, or their covariation.

missing data — the codes used to indicate that respondents' answers to certain questions are lacking because of interviewer or coder error, because of skip patterns of questions, or because respondents did not have opinions on that question.

nonattitude — when respondents really lack an opinion on an issue.

nonprobability designs — samples in which not every person in the population has a known and equal chance of being included.

nonsampling error — all error due to something other than sampling. This includes interviewer effects, question wording effects, and data processing mistakes.

one-way frequencies (also known as **univariate frequencies**) — a display of the distribution and percentage responses to a single question.

open-ended questions — questions where the respondent is not provided with categories to choose from and responses are taken down verbatim by interviewers.

oversample — sampling a subgroup of your sample by a higher sampling fraction to increase that subgroup's sample size and thus decrease the error attached to the analysis of that subgroup. Oversampling can only be done with a stratified or quota sample.

panel poll — a survey that interviews the same people at more than one point in time, usually done to study change and persistence of attitudes.

poll — a systematic, scientific, and impartial way of collecting information from a subset or sample of people, used to generalize to a greater group or population from which that sample is drawn.

population — the complete, relevant group whose attitudes you want to measure accurately in your survey.

precoding — providing categories in the interview that interviewers do not read but use to code the open-ended responses of respondents. This is a subgroup of open-ended questions.

pretest — conducting mock interviews or interviews with respondents like those in your sample (but *not* in the sample) to debug the questionnaire.

probability samples — random samples that give each member of the population a calculable probability or chance of being selected into the sample. Only with probability designs can a survey's accuracy be fully calculated.

probability of selection — the chance of being chosen from the population to be in the sample.

pure random sampling — mixing the names of the population up and choosing them randomly for the sample.

Q by Q — question-by-question explanations provided to the interviewers that give additional clarification and instructions.

quota sampling — a nonprobability sample where interviewers choose respondents with discretion. The limit on this discretion is that certain percentages of the respondents must fall in each of a series of demographic subgroups deemed important for the study to represent the population. For example, the interviewer must interview half women and half men.

random error — nonsystematic variation in the measurement of a concept from true population values. Because such error is not in one direction or another, it does not bias the results.

RDD samples — samples that use randomly generated telephone numbers (i.e., random digit dialing) for the sampling frame.

recoding — changing the initial coding scheme, for example, combining categories to produce for analysis a new set of response categories based on the initial responses to the survey.

replacement sampling — sampling which designates a series of specific sample replacements or alternates for each sample unit.

response error — the difference between the actual attitude or value in the population and the value observed in the survey due to how respondents answer.

response rate — in general, this is the number of interviews completed divided by the total number of individuals or telephone numbers drawn for the sample. In telephone samples of randomly generated telephone numbers, depending on how the sample is drawn, nonworking numbers may be deleted from this base or denominator.

refusal conversion — the procedure in which more experienced interviewers call back respondents who initially refused to do the interview and try to convince them to participate.

sample — the small group you scientifically select and actually interview to measure opinions of the population.

sampling error — error based on the size of the sample, the method of sample selection, and the homogeneity of the population. Calculating the sampling error gives us a range for each of the measured values within which, in our estimation, the population's value truly falls.

sampling fraction — the chance of selection into the population. For a simple random sample, the sampling fraction is calculated as the size of the sample drawn divided by the size of the population.

sampling frame — the list of the population from which the sample is drawn.

short poll — 10-15 minute surveys that assess change over time and the impact of events and strategy and give updates in assessments. Brief interviews.

significant — an observed difference or relationship is said to be significant when it is great enough (given the sample size) not to have occurred simply by chance.

skip patterns — in a series of questions some follow-up questions may not be asked on the basis of responses to previous questions.

spurious relationship — an apparent covariation or association between two concepts or attitudes which in reality is false. The association disappears when you control for the third attitude that is actually causing both of the other two attitudes.

stratification — classifying and dividing the population into subgroups and drawing subsamples from each subgroup to reduce error and ensure a representative sample for each subgroup.

study design — plan of the who, what, where, when, and how of the survey.

study objective — a clear and concise statement of the purpose of the study, survey, or poll. What you want to find out from your survey or study.

subtraction effect — when respondents answer the second, more general, question with reference to the general category minus the part they have already responded to in the first question.

summary statistics — statistics that allow you to determine where people's opinions concentrate and how much variety there is in those opinions.

tracking poll — small, often less procedurally rigid, polls that are conducted within short time periods to trace the development or persistence of certain key opinions.

two-way table (also known as a **cross tabulation**) — a bivariate frequency distribution that shows at the same time the relationship between the responses to two questions.

unfolding technique — interviewing method in which the first question is used to obtain information very broad in nature, and follow-up questions are used to obtain more specific information.

variable — the measure of some concept or characteristic. There are independent variables (the causes) and dependent variables (the effects).

weighting — applies to samples; counting the responses of certain kinds of respondents more or less than once so that the sample will more accurately reflect the known distribution of those kinds of respondents in the population.

wild code — error in the data where respondents are incorrectly coded or keypunched such that they are assigned numbers for their responses that do not exist for that question.

Index

Also Available from Island Press

These titles are available directly from Island Press, Box 7, Covelo, CA 95428. Please enclose $2.75 shipping and handling for the first book and $1.25 for each additional book. California and Washington, DC residents add 6% sales tax. A catalog of current and forthcoming titles is available free of charge. Prices subject to change without notice.

Hazardous Waste Management: Reducing the Risk
By Benjamin A. Goldman, James A. Hulme, and Cameron Johnson for the Council on Economic Priorities

Hazardous Waste Management: Reducing the Risk is a comprehensive sourcebook of facts and strategies which provides the analytic tools needed by policy makers, regulating agencies, hazardous waste generators, and host communities to compare facilities on the basis of site, management, and technology. The Council on Economic Priorities' innovative ranking system applies to real-world, site-specific evaluations, establishes a consistent protocol for multiple applications, assesses relative benefits and risks, and evaluates and ranks ten active facilities and eight leading commercial management corporations.

1986. xx, 316 pp., notes, tables, glossary, index.
Cloth, ISBN 0-933280-30-0. **$64.95**
Paper, ISBN 0-933280-31-9. **$34.95**

An Environmental Agenda for the Future
By Leaders of America's Foremost Environmental Organizations

". . . a substantive book addressing the most serious questions about the future of our resources." — John Chafee, Senator, Environmental & Public Works Committee. "While I am not in agreement with many of the positions the authors take, I believe this book can be the basis for constructive dialogue with industry representatives seeking solutions to environmental problems." — Louis Fernandez, Chairman of the Board, Monsanto Corporation.

The chief executive officers of the ten major environmental and conservation organizations launched a joint venture to examine goals the environmental movement should pursue now and on into the 21st century. This book presents policy recommendations to effect changes needed to bring about a healthier, safer living experience. Issues discussed include: nuclear issues, human population growth, energy strategies, toxic and pollution control, and urban environments.

1985. viii, 155 pp., bibliography.
Paper, ISBN 0-933280-29-7.   **$9.95**

Land-Saving Action
Edited by Russell L. Brenneman and Sarah M. Bates

Land-Saving Action is the definitive guide for conservation practitioners. A written symposium by the 29 leading experts in land conservation. This book presents, in detail, land-saving tools and techniques that have been perfected by individuals and organizations across the nation. This is the first time such information has been available in one volume.

1984. xvi, 249 pp., tables, notes, author biographies, selected readings, index.
Cloth, ISBN 0-933280-23-8.   **$39.95**
Paper, ISBN 0-933280-22-X.   **$24.95**

The Conservation Easement in California
By Thomas S. Barrett and Putnam Livermore for The Trust for Public Land

This is the authoritative legal handbook on conservation easements. This book examines the California law as a model for the nation. It emphasizes the effectiveness and flexibility of the California code. Also covered are the historical and legal backgrounds of easement technology, the state and federal tax implications, and solutions to the most difficult drafting problems.

1983. xiv, 173 pp., appendices, notes, selected bibliography, index.
Cloth, ISBN 0-933280-20-3.   **$34.95**

Private Options: Tools and Concepts for Land Conservation
By Montana Land Reliance and Land Trust Exchange

Techniques and strategies for saving the family farm are presented by 30 experts. *Private Options* details the proceedings of a national conference and brings together, for the first time, the experience and advice of land conservation experts from all over the nation.

1982. xiv, 292 pp., key contacts: resource for local conservation organizations, conference participants, bibliography, index.
Paper, ISBN 0-933280-15-7.   **$25.00**

Community Open Spaces
By Mark Francis, Lisa Cashdan, Lynn Paxson

Over the past decade thousands of community gardens and parks have been developed on vacant neighborhood land in America's major cities. *Community Open Spaces* documents this movement in the U.S. and Europe, explaining how planners, public officials, and local residents can work in their own community to successfully develop open space.

1984. xiv, 250 pp., key contacts: resource organizations, appendices, bibliography, index.
Cloth, ISBN 0-933280-27-0. **$24.95**

Water in the West
By The Western Water Network

An essential reference tool for water managers, public officials, farmers, attorneys, industry officials, and students and professors attempting to understand the competing pressures on our most important natural resource: water.

> Vol. III: *Western Water Flows to the Cities*
> v, 217 pp., maps, table of cases, documents, bibliography, index.
> Paper, **$25.00**

Green Fields Forever: The Conservation Tillage Revolution in America
By Charles E. Little

"Green Fields Forever is a fascinating and lively account of one of the most important technological developments in American agriculture. . . . Be prepared to enjoy an exceptionally well-told tale, full of stubborn inventors, forgotten pioneers, enterprising farmers — and no small amount of controversy." — Kenneth A. Cook, Senior Associate, World Wildlife Fund/Conservation Foundation.

1987. 224 pp., illustrations, appendices, index, bibliography.
Cloth. ISBN 0-933280-35-1. **$24.95**
Paper. ISBN 0-933280-34-3. **$14.95**

Federal Lands: A Guide to Planning, Management, and State Revenues
By Sally K. Fairfax and Carolyn E. Yale

"In most of the western states, natural resource revenues are extremely important as well as widely misunderstood. This book helps to clarify states' dependencies on these revenues, which in some instances may be near-fatal." — Don Snow, Director, Northern Lights Institute. "An invaluable tool for state land managers. Here, in summary, is everything that one needs to know about federal resource management policies." — Rowena Rogers, President, Colorado State Board of Land Commissioners.

1987. xx. 252 pp., charts, maps, bibliography, index.
Paper. ISBN 0-933280-33-5. **$24.95**